How To Claim
The
Abrahamic Covenant

Jay Snell

Jay Snell Evangelistic Association
PO Box 59
Livingston, TX 77351
409-327-3676

FOREWORD BY PAUL F. CROUCH

Are you blessed with everything you need? Are you well in body with no sickness of any kind? Do you have a good job with good income so that you can be a blessing to others? Are your children and loved ones saved and in the Kingdom, and are well in body, soul, and spirit?

IF NOT, THEY CAN BE!

Yes, the covenant and blessings promised to Abraham in Deuteronomy 7:12-15 are ours *if* we will DO and KEEP our part of the covenant or contract! Jay Snell, in this revealing book, shows us HOW to CLAIM these awesome benefits. Not convinced? Well, read it with me:

"And now that we are Christ's we are the true descendants of Abraham, and all of God's promises to him belong to us" (Galations 3:29 TLB).

You will be overwhelmed by these great truths as you learn about God's promises of blessings and provision. Apply them to your own life, and you will never be the same as you learn "How to Claim the Abrahamic Covenant."

Paul F. Crouch
President
Trinity Broadcasting Network

Table of Contents

Chapter One

Why Christians Are Claiming Abrahamic Blessings Now

Hebrew 6:15 says that Abraham "obtained the promise." Verse 14 says the promise he obtained was the promise to be "blessed."

> **Heb. 6:13-15**
> **13 For when God made promise to Abraham, because he could swear by no greater, he sware by himself,**
> **14 Saying, surely blessing I will bless thee, and multiplying I will multiply thee.**
> **15 And so, after he had patiently endured, he obtained the promise. (KJV)**

As I explained in *What Are Abraham's Blessings Anyway?,* the word "bless" means "the beneficial enduement of the power of God to produce well-being in every area of a person's life." Consequently, we proved that the word "bless" contains four things: healing, prosperity, well-being for your family, and salvation for your soul.

Since Abraham obtained the promise of blessing, can we, therefore, provide an Old Testament scripture that demonstrates Abraham's obtaining healing and prosperity? Yes, we can.

Look at Genesis 24:1, which says Abraham was "old, well stricken in age and the Lord had blessed him in all things."

From this passage we learn that no disease or sickness or accident cut him down before his time, for he was "old." Then we learn that he was blessed in all things. In Genesis 24:35 we discover what these "all things" were. His servant said.

Gen 24:35
35 The Lord hath blessed my master greatly, and he
is become great: and he hath given him flocks, and
herds, and silver, and gold, and menservants, and maid-
servants, and camels, and asses. (KJV)

In any culture or society this translates into prosperity and wealth.

In Genesis 25:7-8, we read Abraham lived "an hundred threescore and fifteen years. Then Abraham died in a good old age, an old man, and full of years." Here we see that he lived to be 175 years old. Again, it was a "good" old age. "Good" says to us that his old age was not only prosperous, but was also healthy. How could it be "a good old age" if his body was debilitated by sickness and disease? It could not. We are taught here that his entire life was filled with divine health and prosperity.

Then, in Hebrews 6:11-12, we find a group of Christians who are "inheriting the promises."

Heb 6:11-12
11 And we desire that every one of you do shew the same
diligence to the full assurance of hope unto the end:

12 That ye be not slothful, but followers of them who through faith and patience inherit the promises.
(KJV)

There is a Greek construction here, that does not translate, which tells us that the promises Abraham obtained are the same promises Christians are presently inheriting. In other words, what Abraham obtained, healing and prosperity, is exactly what Christians are presently inheriting.

In Hebrews 6:12, look at the word "inherit." In the Greek, this word is in the present tense. The Greek present tense portrays continuous action in present time. This means that while the author of Hebrews was writing the Epistle to the Hebrews, Christians of his day were even then continuously inheriting the same thing that Abraham obtained. And he obtained healing and prosperity. Think of it. This belongs to you. In *What've They Done With Abraham's Blessings,* and also in *The Unbroken Force of Abraham's Blessings,* I deal at length with Hebrews 6. This is the most faith building chapter in all the Bible. This is the most fantastic passage of scripture on healing and prosperity I know about.

But, you might ask, if Christians are presently inheriting Abraham's blessings of healing and prosperity, then why don't I have them? And, how do I get them? The answer is we have to "fight the good fight of faith." But what is faith and how do I fight it?

I believe we have missed a big "something" concerning faith. And we certainly have missed another big "something" when it comes to "fighting" the good fight of faith. Most of us don't realize that we must fight at all. We feel that if we have "faith" that God just sends the great white bird to fly over our house and drop our sack of gold right into our yard. This is not how God operates. We must have

7

the "Abrahamic Faith." And we must wage a warfare the same way they did in the Old Testament. Then we will have what Abraham obtained. There is no other way.

What Abraham obtained is also your right as a Christian because you were included in The Abrahamic Covenant right along with Abraham himself. In the balance of this chapter, I want to show you two things. First, I want to show you that you were indeed included in the promises of wealth (and health) right along with Abraham and are entitled to wealth just as much as Abraham was. Second, I want to show you the two basic things Abraham did to "begin and maintain" the flow of wealth from God to himself. Then, in the remaining chapters, we shall see how you too can open up the flow of provision from God to yourself.

The Abrahamic Covenant is composed of sixty promises that God made to Abraham. Of those sixty promises, Gentile Christians are included in at least thirteen of them.

Promise #8

> **Gen 12:3**
> **3 And I will bless them that bless thee, and curse him that curseth thee: and in thee shall all families of the earth be blessed. (KJV)**

Promise #60

> **Gen 22:18**
> **18 And in thy seed shall all the nations of the earth be blessed; because thou hast obeyed my voice. (KJV)**

In these two promises, obviously, "families" and "nations" included more than just the physical seed of Abraham (Jews, Hebrews or Israelites). In addition, these non-Jews or Gentiles, are tied up with the word "bless."

As stated previously, this word contains four things: healing, prosperity, well-being for the families of those so blessed, and salvation for their souls.

Consequently, when we see that we are "blessed" in the very same Abrahamic Covenant right along with Abraham himself, and when we see that "bless" includes tremendous wealth, it becomes easy to see why the author of Hebrews tells us that Christians are presently, continuously inheriting and receiving Abrahamic Blessings.

Next, we must determine what two things Abraham did to "begin and maintain" the flow of these blessings from heaven to himself. We shall identify these two things first. Then, we shall make note that these two things are a "power" given by God himself to Abraham for the purpose of claiming God's promises.

We shall also note that this "power" has been extended to Abraham's people, now composed of both Jew and Gentile. In this work, we shall refer to Abraham's people as *The Abrahamic Seed Group.*

Abraham's First Step To Receiving The Promises

The first of the two things that he did to "begin and maintain" the flow of provision to himself was ***he gave a tithe.*** This record has been kept for us in two places.

Gen 14:18-20

18 And Melchizedek king of Salem brought forth bread and
wine: and he was the priest of the most high God.
19 And he blessed him, and said, Blessed be Abram of the most
high God, possessor of heaven and earth:
20 And blessed be the most high God, which hath delivered
thine enemies into thy hand. And he gave him tithes of all.
(KJV)

Heb 7:1-4

1 For this Melchisedec, king of Salem, priest of the most high
God, who met Abraham returning from the slaughter of the kings,
and blessed him;
2 To whom also Abraham gave a tenth part of all; first being
by interpretation King of righteousness, and after that also King of
Salem, which is, King of peace;
3 Without father, without mother, without descent, having
neither beginning of days, nor end of life; but made like unto the
Son of God; abideth a priest continually.
4 Now consider how great this man was, unto whom even the
patriarch Abraham gave the tenth of spoils.
(KJV)

Note well at this point that there was no command nor law from God
for Abraham to tithe. Moses' law had not come into being yet nor
would it for nearly four hundred more years. Yet, Abraham paid
tithes to Melchizedek, the high priest of God. Why? Did Abraham
know something that some people haven't learned to this day?

Abraham's Second Step To Receiving The Promises

The second thing Abraham did to "start and maintain" the flow of
blessing and provision was *to make offerings in addition to his tithe.*
We know he made offerings from the fact that at least three times in
his life, he built an altar.

Gen 12:7-8

7 And the LORD appeared unto Abram, and said, Unto thy seed will I give this land: and there builded he an altar unto the LORD, who appeared unto him.

8 And he removed from thence unto a mountain on the east of Bethel, and pitched his tent, having Bethel on the west, and Hai on the east: and there he builded an altar unto the LORD, and called upon the name of the LORD.

(KJV)

Gen 13:18

18 Then Abram removed his tent, and came and dwelt in the plain of Mamre, which is in Hebron, and built there an altar unto the LORD.

(KJV)

Gen 22:9

9 And they came to the place which God had told him of; and Abraham built an altar there and laid the wood in order, and bound Isaac his son, and laid him on the altar upon the wood.

(KJV)

Early in the Old Testament, an altar was a place prepared for sacrificing by slaughter in the form of an offering to God. The same altar could be used several times for the same purpose.

In addition to Abraham, his son Isaac, the first member of *The Abrahamic Seed Group,* added one more altar to the four that Abraham had built. This altar was located in Beersheba,

Gen 26:24-25

24 And the LORD appeared unto him the same night, and said, I am the God of Abraham thy father; fear not, for I am with thee, and will bless thee, and multiply thy seed for my servant Abraham's sake.

25 And he builded an altar there, and called upon the name of the LORD, and pitched his tent there: and there Isaac's servants digged a well.
(KJV)

Finally, Jacob, the third member of *The Abrahamic Seed Group,* restored for his own use two of the altars that Abraham, his grandfather, had built. This restoration occurred in two places in the sacred record.

Gen 33:20
20 And he erected there an altar, and called it El-elohe-Israel.
(KJV)

Gen 35:1-3
1 And God said unto Jacob, Arise, go up to Bethel, and dwell there: and make there an altar unto God, that appeared unto thee when thou fleddest from the face of Esau thy brother.
2 Then Jacob said unto his household, and to all that were with him, put away the strange gods that are among you, and be clean, and change your garments:
3 And let us arise, and go up to Bethel; and I will make there an altar unto God, who answered me in the day of my distress, and was with me in the way which I went.
(KJV)

Now, why did Abraham tithe and give offerings when there was no command nor law from God ordering him to do so? The answer might be that Abraham was nobody's fool. He recognized the *Law of Sowing and Reaping.* After all, he saw it constantly operate in nature. He saw it operate in agriculture. He saw it operate in livestock. He saw it continually. If you sow properly, you will also reap bountifully. This was his everyday experience. Therefore, being nobody's fool, he could have reasoned that if he wanted a financial harvest, all he had to do was tap the *Law of Sowing and Reaping* with his material possessions, just like he did with everything else.

But, is there not something wrong with this reasoning? Yes, very definitely. But, what? *The Law of Sowing and Reaping,* with which Abraham was familiar, involved something with life in it; that is, something which had the capacity to reproduce, such as livestock or an agricultural seed of wheat, cotton, corn, etc. But, material wealth such as a precious metal, gemstone, money, etc., is inanimate. These items lack life. They cannot reproduce themselves. Consequently, was Abraham *only* looking at the *Law of Sowing and Reaping* when he paid tithes and gave offerings when God had not placed a requirement upon him to do so? Could it not have been that he was indeed looking to the sowing and reaping law but *only after it had been combined with an added power from God which made inanimate things reproduce themselves?*

Notice again the definition of the term "bless." It means the "beneficial enduement of the *Power of God to Produce* well-being in every area of a person's life." *The Power of God to Produce!*

Abraham linked the *Law of Sowing and Reaping,* with which he was familiar, to God's main, covenant promise to "bless him" in all things. As a result, when he sowed, *God supernaturally added the power inherent in "bless" to his sowing, and inanimate things supernaturally reproduced themselves many times over.* No wonder Abraham tithed and gave offerings even when God did not require it of him.

More proof of this will be seen specifically in the chapter on tithing and the chapter on giving offerings. We shall see in the tithing section, that there are *seven supernatural power things which happen* when a person tithes.

In the section on giving, we shall see that the very thing a person gives is also the very thing that God *supernaturally powers up to come back to the giver multiplied many times over.* It is as though what you gave was never given to start with.

The Law of Sowing and Reaping **combined** with God's *supernatural power* inherent in "bless" gives us the true meaning of Deuteronomy 8:17-18.

> **Deut 8:17-18**
> **17 And thou say in thine heart, My power and the might of mine hand hath gotten me this wealth.**
> **18 But thou shalt remember the LORD thy God: for it is he that giveth thee power to get wealth, that he may establish his covenant which he sware unto thy fathers, as it is this day.**
> **(KJV)**

The covenant spoken of here is The Abrahamic Covenant. We know this for two reasons. First, we know it is The Abrahamic Covenant because of the expression "thy fathers." When this expression is used, it always refers to Abraham, Isaac and Jacob. The covenant was made with Abraham, then God confirmed it to both Isaac and Jacob.

The second reason is because of the word translated from Hebrew into our English word "establish." This makes the meaning appear to be that God had set up something new at that point in time and was about to establish it with them then and there. But, this is not the meaning of this word in this context. Its meaning here is "continue." It is a fact that God "established" The Abrahamic Covenant with them then and there, but He did it by way of just "continuing" what He began with Abraham and confirmed with both Isaac and Jacob.

In other words, God "established by continuance" The Abrahamic Covenant with those living at that time who were members of *The Abrahamic Seed Group*. This word is also translated in the KJV of the Bible by our English word "confirm," which means the same thing in this context as "continue." As a matter of fact, both the NAS and the NIV versions of the Bible translate it by "confirm" in this very passage.

Below we list some scriptures which demonstrates the various ways this Hebrew word is translated. These will suffice to show you that this word does in fact mean that God simply confirmed, performed, caused to stand and continue The Abrahamic Covenant with those living members of *The Abrahamic Seed Group.*

These passages show the word translated by "stand."

> **Num 30:4-5**
> 4 And her father hear her vow, and her bond wherewith she hath bound her soul, and her father shall hold his peace at her: then all her vows shall stand, and every bond wherewith she hath bound her soul shall stand.
> 5 But if her father disallow her in the day that he heareth; not any of her vows, or of her bonds wherewith she hath bound her soul, shall stand: and the LORD shall forgive her, because her father disallowed her.
> **(KJV)**

> **Num 30:7**
> 7 And her husband heard it, and held his peace at her in the day that he heard it: then her vows shall stand, and her bonds wherewith she bound her soul shall stand. **(KJV)**

> **Num 30:9**
> 9 But every vow of a widow, and of her that is divorced, wherewith they have bound their souls, shall stand against her. **(KJV)**

15

Num 30:11-12

11 And her husband heard it, and held his peace at her, and disallowed her not: then all her vows shall stand, and every bond wherewith she bound her soul shall stand.

12 But if her husband hath utterly made them void on the day he heard them; then whatsoever proceeded out of her lips concerning her vows, or concerning the bond of her soul, shall not stand: her husband hath made them void; and the LORD shall forgive her (KJV)

This passage shows the word translated by "confirm."

Deut 27:2 6

26 Cursed be he that confirmeth not all the words of this law to do them. And all the people shall say, Amen. (KJV)

These passages translated it by "perform."

1 Sam 3:12

12 In that day I will perform against Eli all things which I have spoken concerning his house: when I begin, I will also make an end. (KJV)

1 Sam 15:11

11 It repenteth me that I have set up Saul to be king: for he is turned back from following me, and hath not performed my commandments. And it grieved Samuel; and he cried unto the LORD all night. (KJV)

1 Sam 15:13

13 And Samuel came to Saul: and Saul said unto him, Blessed be thou of the LORD. I have performed the commandment of the Lord. (KJV)

1 King 6:12

12 Concerning this house which thou art in building, if thou wilt walk in my statutes, and execute my judgements, and keep all my commandments to walk in them; then will I perform my word with thee, which I spake unto David thy father... (KJV)

16

These passages translate it by "continue."

> **1 Sam 13:14**
> 14 But now thy kingdom shall not continue: the LORD hath
> sought him a man after his own heart, and the LORD hath com-
> manded him to be captain over his people, because thou hast not
> kept that which the LORD commanded thee. (KJV)

> **1 King 2:4**
> 4 That the LORD may continue his word which he spake con-
> cerning me, saying, if thy children take heed to their way, to walk
> before me in truth with all their heart and with all their soul, there
> shall not fail thee (said he) a man on the throne of Israel. (KJV)

From the preceding God is simply saying to *The Abrahamic Seed
Group* that he is going to cause The Abrahamic Covenant to "stand"
for them. As such, He "confirmed" it for them by "continuing" to
"perform" it in their behalf.

What specific thing did God say He was going to do that would
enable them to know that He had indeed continued The Abrahamic
Covenant with them? *He said that He was giving them power to get
wealth for the specific purpose of continuing the Covenant with
them.* The power to get wealth was the only thing given to us for us
to know that He has, of a certainty, continued the Abrahamic system
with us as it is at this day.

Look at the word "power" which is used twice in Deuteronomy 8:17-
18. It is the same Hebrew word in both verses, but it is used in two
distinct ways. In verse 17 it is used concerning man's *natural abilities.* But, in verse 18 this word "power" is used concerning God's
supernatural abilities. Now, this concept of supernatural ability and
power of God is the very heart of The Abrahamic Covenant.

17

"Bless" means "the supernatural ability and power of God *to produce well-being in every area of their lives.* And, this "well-being" includes four things: healing, prosperity, well-being for their families in addition to the salvation of their soul. In other words, *God had to give them the blessing power to get wealth because he promised it to The Abrahamic Seed Group in His covenant with Abraham.* He had no choice. He must keep His word. He must do what He promised. So he gave us the Abrahamic power to get wealth.

We need not think that all this means is that God will bless their crops and herds, making them more productive than usual. This is certainly contained within the borders of "bless" in The Abrahamic Covenant. But, much more is included in Deuteronomy 8:17-18. Contained within its perimeters lies the *power of God to produce,* which enables inanimate, lifeless objects and things to reproduce themselves just as though they had life inherent in them.

This was true of the deadness of Abraham's body after child bearing age. Paul said in Romans 4:17 that "God giveth life to the dead, and calleth those things which are not, as though they were...." But what was true concerning Abraham's body is also true of tithing and offering inanimate, lifeless pieces of money. With the *supernatural, Abrahamic blessing power* God promised and gave in His covenant with Abraham, He gives life to the inanimate money when you tithe it and give it in the form of offerings so that it reproduces itself. How else can you explain it?

Anyone who has made a lifestyle, as Abraham did, of tithing and giving offerings will tell you by their own experience that God supernaturally multiplies what they gave so that they ultimately have more than what they had beforehand. But, why is this so? How can an inanimate, lifeless object like a piece of money reproduce itself? All the above is the answer to this question. *Tithing and giving offerings causes a supernatural reproduction of what you "sowed," and this supernatural ability to reproduce was given to us by God in order to "continue" The Abrahamic Covenant with us.* In addition to his love for God, this is the reason Abraham paid tithes and gave offerings.

As we explore this concept further in the pages of this book, you will see that this Abrahamic power belongs to you just as much as it did to Abraham himself. You will also see for yourself that the blessings associated with it still supernaturally produce today for you just as much as they did in the years of the Old Testament. God wants you to be extremely blessed, and I am about to prove it for you.

Chapter Two

The First Step You Must Take
To Claim Abrahamic Blessings

You can go to man's school and study man's economics or you can go to God's school and study God's economics. I choose to do it God's way. I have found that it works. It keeps on working. It never fails. There is no power on earth that can blow it out of the battle. I just keep doing business God's way. If I am lined up with God, we make a majority. As long as God and I are a majority I will charge hell with a squirt gun, if He says so, knowing that I can put it out. God is bigger than anything anybody can hurl at Him. So I just believe in doing business God's way; whether its economics or whatever.

Therefore, I want to show you some things about how to get ahead financially, and stay ahead. So if you want a Ph.D. in God's finance, stick around. I am going to give you the principle whereby you don't have to worry about getting your needs met financially.

I want you to see first of all that God made some promises to a fellow named Abraham. Those promises were healing, prosperity, well-being for his family, in addition to the salvation of his soul. Those promises also included Abraham's seed which includes the physical descendants of Abraham.

But you and I in the Christian era are grafted into that same Abrahamic system because we also are Abraham's seed. We are *The Abrahamic Seed Group*. I hear all this stuff about the "church." But, the "church" must remember we are the "seed of Abraham" (Gal 3:29).

Who makes up the church? Abraham's seed, that's who. You must be a member of the Abrahamic Seed Group to be a part of the church. Therefore, we are the church, because we are Abraham's seed. When we start thinking in that term, we will see that we are entitled to more than what modern theology will give to us by their modern term "church," because most modern theologians want to start us off at Pentecost. The Bible starts us off with Abraham in Genesis 12. So what God promised Abraham is in fact promised to us also.

Now, I want to show you some things about Abraham and tithing. This is going to startle you since Abraham was one of the richest men in the world because God made him rich. *Abraham tithed even though God never commanded him to.* As a matter of fact, there was no law or scripture in Abraham's day which said, "Thou shalt tithe." You want proof of that? Look at Hebrews chapter 7, verses 1 and 2.

> **Heb 7:1-2**
> **1 For this Melchisedec, king of Salem, priest of the most high God, who met Abraham returning from the slaughter of the kings, and blessed him;**
> **2 To whom also Abraham gave a tenth part of all; first being by interpretation King of righteousness, and after that also King of Salem, which is, King of peace;**
> **(KJV)**

This high priest, Melchisdec, met Abraham returning from one of the battles and he blessed him. Then the next verse says, "to this man Abraham gave the tithe or the tenth part of all." Here is

Abraham paying tithes to the high priest of God, but there was no scripture or command of God at that time in history that demanded that Abraham pay tithes at all. As a matter of fact, there was nothing in the Bible at this point that said a fellow ought to tithe, nothing. No command, nowhere, that made a man tithe, but here is the priest of the most high God who meets somebody as important as Abraham, and Abraham tithed to him anyway.

The question is, why did he do it? If he was not commanded to do it, why did he do it? Because Abraham was a sharp business man. He was one of the best. If you have aspirations to start and run your own business, you'd surely do well to pattern it after this man called Abraham.

Seven Wealth Building Things Supernaturally Produced by God's Abrahamic Blessing Power For The One Who Tithes

Why did Abraham start tithing? I want to show you some things. Go to the book of Malachi. We are going to see that there are seven specific blessings that come to the man who tithes. Now somebody says, "You are using an Old Testament scripture." You are right. "Well, that's pertaining to the Jews." You are right again. "Then, that does not apply to us."

You are wrong. Why? Because this is written to the Abrahamic Seed Group. During the Old Testament era, it pertained to just the Jews. But when Christ came and died we Gentile Christians were grafted into the same identical Abrahamic System, because we are *The Abrahamic Seed Group.* Therefore, what it says to *The Abrahamic Seed Group* in one place, pertains to *The Abrahamic*

Seed Group in another place. So what is said here applies to every Christian reading this page.

What you have to do is figure out if you are Abraham's Seed or not. If you are, this applies to you. I am a member of *The Abrahamic Seed Group*. Therefore, I put myself right in the middle of this scripture, and guess what? It works for me, too. Because I am in *Abraham's Seed Group* and this was written to *The Abrahamic Seed Group*. Therefore, the same seven blessings from God that Malachi presented to the people of that day, are still valid for us Gentile Christians now.

Now, what are the seven blessings? I asked a while ago why did Abraham tithe when he didn't have to? Moses' Law demanded the people to tithe. But, Moses' Law didn't even come into being until over 400 years later. He tithed when he didn't have to. So the law that said "Thou shalt tithe," didn't even exist in Abraham's day. But here we have Abraham, the father of us all, tithing when he didn't have to. If he tithed when he didn't have to, there had to be a good reason on the part of Abraham to do it. Well, there was. Abraham recognized the benefits for the person who paid tithes. Now here is what Abraham found as penned hundreds of years later by Malachi.

> **Mal 3:10-12**
> **10 Bring ye all the tithes into the storehouse, that there may be meat in mine house, and prove me now herewith, saith the LORD of hosts, if I will not open you the windows of heaven, and pour you out a blessing, that there shall not be room enough to receive it.**
> **11 And I will rebuke the devourer for your sakes, and he shall not destroy the fruits of your ground; neither shall your vine cast her fruit before the time in the field, saith the LORD of hosts.**
> **12 And all nations shall call you blessed: for ye shall be a delightsome land, saith the LORD of hosts. (KJV)**

Notice verse 10 says "Bring all the tithes into the storehouse that there may be meat [or food] in my house and test me now by this" saith the LORD, "if I will not do seven fantastic things for you." (The "storehouse" and "my house" is where you get fed, whether your church, a book and tape ministry, TBN, a missionary, or a combination of the above). God here asks us to test Him by doing one thing and then watching Him do seven things in response to it.

To my knowledge, this is the only place in scripture where we are asked or even challenged to test God on an issue. He says, "Test Me in this act and see that your bringing the tithe to My storehouse will cause Me to return seven things to you." A seven for one return, and He says, "Test Me in this"! I don't know of any other place in scripture where God issues a specific challenge saying, "Test Me in a specific matter." Here He is saying for us to do one thing and check Him out. "Test Me. I am going to do seven things in return."

Now does that sound like a pretty good return? In this day of meager rates of return on your savings accounts in your bank, if you found a place that had an iron clad guarantee that would pay you back seven times more than you put in, and you had confidence in the bank and the banker, would you take your money out of an account where they were paying you only 3 1/2% and place it in the place where they would give you 700%? That just makes good sense, doesn't it?

Was Abraham a good businessman or not? You see he has a good deal going here. God says test me now by this and see if I won't do seven things for you in return for you doing the one thing for me, which is bringing in the tithe.

25

The First Provision Building Thing Supernaturally Produced By God's Abrahamic Blessing Power For The One Who Tithes

What are these seven things? First of all, look back at verse 10. Here it is. "I will open for you the windows of heaven." Now I want you to look at that part specifically where it says, "I will open for you." This blesses me. Why? Because I have seen the time when I needed something opened for me. I mean there have been times in my life when I didn't need generalities. I needed somebody to get down here where I live, where my need is now, where I hurt today and get real and get specific with me. Now, it wouldn't bless me as much if He said, "I will open the windows for you *all,*" as it does the way He said it. He said "I will open the windows for *you.*"

When He says "you," He means the one that is doing the tithing. Well, I am a tither. As a matter of fact, I do more that that. And so God said first of all I am going to open for "you," the tither, the windows of heaven. Well what does that signify for me?

I view heaven as being the source of everything I need. The Bible says, "My God shall supply all your needs according to His riches in glory through Jesus Christ." Now according to this, the Father, Christ and riches are all up there in heaven. Therefore, I need *that* window opened for me.

Well, He says, "Try it. Test Me. I will open the windows of heaven for you." Do you see that? That's for *The Abraham Seed Group* when they tithe. I am showing you what Abraham saw, what Melchisedec saw. Abraham was one of the most blessed men in the world, because he learned to live according to God's covenant.

The Second Provision Building Thing Supernaturally Produced By God's Abrahamic Blessing Power For The One Who Tithes

Now notice the second thing. Not only are the windows of heaven opened, but notice, *"I will pour out for you a blessing."* I want you to look at the word "blessing." When you find that word coming from God to any member of *The Abraham Seed Group* here is what the word means: **the beneficial enduement of God's power to produce well-being in every area of a person's life.** The word "blessing" comes from the Hebrew word "barak" translated by the Greek word "eulogia" and translated into English by our word "bless." Bless means the beneficial enduement of God's **power to produce well-being** in every area of a person's life.

When He says, "I will open heaven's window and pour you out a blessing," He is saying, "I will pour out upon you my beneficial **power to produce** well-being in whatever area your need is." Now that gets strong, my friend. This is exactly what the word **bless** means in Hebrew, Greek and English when it pertains to the relationship between the Abrahamic Covenant, the God of that covenant, and *The Abrahamic Seed Group.* I trigger this **blessing** by my tithing.

Do you begin to see why Abraham figured this thing out even when God had not said, "Thou shalt tithe"? He didn't have to. If you get this kind of thing going, who has to "command" you to do it? It's like you have $100 in savings in your bank but another bank is paying 700% interest while your bank is only paying 3 1/2% interest.

Nobody has to put a gun to your head and say, "Thou shalt move

27

your money to the bank which pays 700% interest." Why? Because it makes sense. Now, I will open the windows of heaven and pour you out a beneficial enduement of my (God's) *power to produce* whatever your need is. That's what that word "blessing" means. We trigger that "blessing" by starting to give in the form of the tithe.

Nobody had to tell Abraham to tithe. Once he figured this thing out, nobody could stop him. ***It's not that we have to tithe. It's that we get to.*** If you are part of *The Abraham Seed Group,* everything I am saying here pertains to you. And this *blessing* return pertains to you. In my days as a Baptist minister, I didn't know about the "blessing" part of this. I would preach tithing from the standpoint of the law. I would preach, "Thou shalt tithe. Anybody who is not going to tithe is next to going to hell, probably are anyhow." You know, I could tighten the screws down better and put a Gentile Christian under the Law better than any Baptist preacher you ever heard. But, when God began to show me other things, I got into the deeper things of God and I said, "Lord, I missed all of this for so long." Why, if you present it the way it really is, *you can't stop people from tithing.* Because I see the seven blessings involved with it, I am going to tithe. You can't stop me from tithing. I do more than the tithe, and I am as blessed as anybody. Yes, God says "I will pour you out a blessing."

The Third Provision Building Thing Supernaturally Produced By God's Abrahamic Blessing Power For The One Who Tithes

Notice the third thing. "There shall not be room enough to receive it." I am so grateful that God does not deal in smallness. Being the father of two girls, I discovered that girls are different and special.

There is something about a little girl that can wrap a Dad right around her little finger. Sure, we Dads could pinch their heads off sometimes, because they can do that to us. But when it comes to my family, my daughters, my two granddaughters, and two grandsons, I just give and give and give. That's just my nature; I just give. They never have to worry about me putting limits on my giving to them. Let me illustrate this.

The other day my oldest granddaughter, Haley, who is six, wanted her Paw Paw to take her to Chucky Cheese's. She wanted me to take just me and her, by herself. Well, I knew what was coming. She was putting the con on me big time. You see, if her baby sister, Amber, age three, is along, well that sort of splits up the loot that she gets from me. Now, you know I wasn't born yesterday. I knew what was coming. But I am a sucker for this little girl. That's just the way I am. And they learn this, the little brats. I mean they have learned me. So I said OK. So I and the oldest little granddaughter go to Chucky Cheese's.

Well, she is a smart little thing, and she likes to play the games. The little one likes to ride the rides; the oldest one likes to play the games. She has learned which games she can beat. When you do well on the games, they give out tickets, and she has learned the ones that she does best on.

So, she plays those particular ones over and over and over. She has about three or four that she can just beat big time. Man, she comes out with all these tickets, then she will go over and trade them for a prize. My point is this, there are no limits to what her grandpa will do for that baby.

Notice what God says. I will pour out a blessing: that beneficial enduement of power to produce, and it will be so big you won't have room enough to receive it. My granddaughter got 170 tickets the other day at Chucky Cheese's, which cost her Paw Paw plenty, but my baby girl had the time of her life, let me tell you. She said, "I know you love me Paw Paw, because you buy me things." I said, "Thanks a million little girl." You see, she knows how this "Paw Paw business" is put together.

Well, God has promised that our blessing will be so big that there will not be room enough to receive it. Usually we tell the kids it is time to go, we've got to go, let's go. I didn't do that this time. I let her play those games. I was determined to let her play them until I ran out of money or she got so tired she was about to drop and say let's go home. Well, the two happened about the same time, because when she got tired and said let's go, I think maybe I had one more dollar in my pocket. So it was time to go.

That's how God is. He said the blessing will be so large you won't have room to receive it. You are beginning to see why Abraham got in on tithing. You see, Abraham had a heart and a mind for God. He didn't need a law which told him to tithe.

Abraham was just so close to God and he trusted God to the point where he saw the seven blessings involved with tithing to God. As a matter of fact, Abraham found out that you can't beat God no matter what you do. So, he began to tithe.

He gave tithes to this high priest named Melchisedec, and the blessings began to flow. He saw that, even though there was not a law which commanded it, this is how it is supposed to be done.

Four hundred and twenty years later Moses came, and God incorporated tithing into the law. Why did he do that? To be mean to people? No, to enable them to maintain the seven blessings God promised all of us in The Abrahamic Covenant.

The Fourth Provision Building Thing Supernaturally Produced By God's Abrahamic Blessing Power For The One Who Tithes

Let's look at verse 11. "I will rebuke the devourer for your sakes." Now, that's the devil. The devourer is the devil. The devil will never let up on you. There are some things that we need to come to grips with that we can't do. The sooner we come to grips with those things, stop trying, and turn it over to God and let Him do it His way, the better off we will be. You cannot beat the devil on your own. Now you just can't do that. I understand our authority. I preach it. I understand our power. I wrote a book on it entitled *How To Exercise God's Megaton Power Now.* So I understand authority and power. I understand the use of the name of Jesus because God has revealed all of that to me. But the point is, we have to have these instruments, or whatever you want to call them, in order to deal with the devil because we can't beat him on our own.

But there is a blanket insurance policy that we can have from God against the devourer which stops him from devouring what's ours, and that insurance policy is tithing. Notice what He said. He said, "Bring all the tithes into the store house and prove me now herewith." One of the seven power blessings that He gives which proves Him is this: He actually rebukes the devourer for our sakes. "I will rebuke him!" God is the One Who dresses the devil down and makes him get out of my face. God is the One Who provides protection for me, who runs interference between me and the devil and stops him from walking all over me. The devil will hurt you. He will take your health. He will take your finances. He will wreck your home. He will destroy your marriage. He will steal your job.

31

He will break and tear up everything good that you have going for you, if God does not stop him. But tithing brings the fulfillment of "I will rebuke the devourer for your sakes."

Some years ago a person gave me a brand new car which had leather seats, CD player, the whole bit. But there were strings on that automobile. This person wanted to dictate to me. He wanted to dictate to the church that I pastored. I had to deal with this person, shut him down, and get rid of those strings. Nobody can ever be allowed to sit in that kind of position over any man of God. That's just out. You know, either we follow the leadership of a person like that or we follow God, because the two don't wind up in the same place. So you have to make up your mind quickly, and then go in that direction. So he took my car. But I never had to walk for one day. God rebuked the devourer by providing me with a beautiful little sports car.

I will rebuke the devourer. Brother, I have had all sorts of things thrown at me, but I always win. I do not lose. I have never lost. I have been set back but I don't lose. They say the key is to learn how to be a good loser. That's "baloney." I am not going to be a good loser. I am going to scratch and kick and fight the whole way. Because when I lose the devourer has gotten the upper hand, and I don't like that. So I am not a good sport. Not at all, because God said, "I will rebuke the devourer for your sake." Do you see it? And He said, "prove Me by this." So just start tithing. Is it any wonder Abraham was a tither?

The Fifth Provision Building Thing Supernaturally Produced By God's Abrahamic Blessing Power For Those Who Tithe

Furthermore, God promises that your vine shall not cast his fruit before the time in the field. Now, the background there is agriculture, but you can fit it to anything in the world. Notice, what He says here. "He shall not destroy the fruits of your ground." Now, I don't care what kind of ground you are working in. Maybe you are a doctor, lawyer, Indian chief, gas pumper, ditch digger, house painter, it makes no difference.

However you make your way, that's your ground. As part of the Abrahamic Seed Group, you have some ground. Now, the Bible says that if you start tithing, God is going to stop the devil from messing with your fruit. Did you ever have a setback in the way you are making a living? Brother, get your tithe lined up and God will get between that setback and you. He will begin to deal with that setback stuff and will run some interference for you so that the devil can neither puncture nor penetrate. Glory to God!

The Sixth Provision Building Thing Supernaturally Produced By God's Abrahamic Blessing Power For Those Who Tithe

Notice something else. Not only does He stop him from destroying your fruit, but He deals with the vine. God even deals with the vine, the very source. Sometimes the vine has a tendency to get a blight or disease in it and make the grape turn loose before its actual time. The Bible says that God will deal not just with the devourer, who wants to mess with the fruit of the vine, but that He will deal with the vine so that the vine itself cannot dump your crop before you have the time or the opportunity to harvest it.

I believe that when a man throws the seed in his field, he ought to be allowed to harvest it and so does God. Here is the crux of this thing. When you don't tithe, you *are eating your seed.* You cannot reap what you have not sown. If you take your seed and eat it, you cannot sow it to reap a bigger harvest. You see, all this stuff just fits and make sense.

Now all of this is what God said. I didn't say it. What He said here applies to you. If you have been saved you are the Seed of Abraham, and that's the group He is talking about here. He is speaking these promises to the Seed of Abraham, and He said you bring the tithes in, Seed of Abraham, and prove me by that action, if I won't do seven beneficial power things for you. Then He begins to list them.

The Seventh Provision Building Thing Supernaturally Produced By God's Abrahamic Blessing Power For Those Who Tithe

Finally, He says all nations shall call you blessed for you shall be a delightsome land. Now, how can their land be delightsome if, in fact, God has not blessed that land? You want to be well thought of in your land, on your job, because "your land" is that sphere of God's creation through which you make your way, your living. Now, you want to be well thought of on your land? You want to get the promotions? You want all nations to call you blessed because you are a delightsome land, then begin to tithe, dear brother. God will establish your reputation in the minds of other people.

We sometimes read things inadequately. We just skim it, and it doesn't mean much to us because we don't stop and think about it. The person that does not tithe cannot possibly be experiencing these blessings. That type of person usually wishes the pastor or preacher would speak on a different subject. I have been there. I know how you feel. But my point to you is this, God said, "prove Me now

34

herewith." Now there is a challenge. So I challenge you. Try it God's way one year and see at the end of the year where you are. I can tell you, you are going to be way ahead of where you are now. Why? Because you will be able to keep more of what you make or earn because God is going to begin running interference for you and rebuke the devourer off your earnings.

So, I am challenging you like God did. Notice what He said, "prove Me now herewith." Can you see this? Prove Me now by this, literally, is what that says. See if I will not open for you the windows of heaven. Keep noticing the places in here, where He says over and over and over, it's *your* ground, it's *your* vine, it's *your* field, it's *your* sakes, pour out for *you*. The emphasis in this passage is upon the concept *you* and *yours*. He uses that expression over and over and over in these two verses. Put your name in these two verses because you belong there. This is said to you. If you are saved, you are The Seed of Abraham. This is spoken to The Seed of Abraham.

But, you may say that this is purely Old Testament. Nonsense. We Gentile Christians have been grafted into that Old Testament *Abrahamic Seed Group* bunch on an equal footing with them. Consequently, we are lined up with everything in The Abrahamic Covenant that God said to them. These promises belong to us also. Hallelujah. Enough of this business of declaring that's Old Testament and this is New Testament. It is all *The Abrahamic Seed Group* - period. What it says in one place to this group it means in another place also. We are all, us today, together with them *The Abrahamic Seed Group*. Therefore, this passage of scripture applies to you and me today.

Well, when are you going to start? Abraham had it together. Abraham didn't need somebody to get up and preach him a sermon.

He figured this thing out for himself and tested the waters a little bit at a time. Finally, he launched out and when Melchisedec came along, he paid tithes to that man of God right there on the spot and the whole thing just started coming his way. And it will work for you. I have never seen the guy that was a tither ever wind up on the short end of the heap. Never, never, in my life have I seen that.

As a Christian I have been on both sides of the tithing issue. My great problem is my mind, just as your great problem is your mind. We have analytical minds. We can figure out too much. Many times we don't need God. We are too smart. We will figure that thing out. We can do this. We can make that move. We can do something else and yet it will work short term. But, we get no insurance that God is going to run interference for us long term, unless we do it His way short term. And so the guy that determines to do it God's way short term has God's protection long term.

Start now doing it God's way, and you will still be here when the Johnny Come Latelies and the Flashes in the Pans and the Skyrockets have fizzled and their lights have gone out. You are going to still be here blessed, prosperous and wealthy.

There used to be some people in my church, a man and his wife, who came in there and took their place on the front row. They had their same two seats and they put their Bibles on them. She put hers here. He put his there. They would leave them there, indicating "this chair is my chair." So they would leave them there. They wouldn't take them home. When they came back, nobody, of course, would sit in that chair because it had somebody's Bible in it. After two or three weeks of that, everybody just knew that was their chair. I don't know if they ever read their Bible or not. I do know it was a marker, i.e., a property marker. So they had their chairs, having staked their claims with their property-marking Bibles. Then, this guy would come up on the platform. Well, I never asked him up on the platform. I never asked him up there a time. But he would come up to make an announcement. He was always putting together a work group for the people in the church and so they would come to the church to work. He would line out the work for them to do, and then he would take off, he wouldn't work. He would line it out for all the others, but he wouldn't do a thing but play big shot.

Well, this is a "Skyrocket." But in looking over the records, this guy did not tithe. But he could line all of this work stuff up for the rest of us. He could and did put his property-marker Bible down over there. Well, I had to deal with him. So he left. Our offerings did not go down a bit. You see he didn't make any offerings so how could our offerings go down when he left? He wasn't doing it God's way to start with. You know, if he would have done it God's way, he wouldn't have had to mark off his chair with his Bible, because God would have made everybody see what a great Christian he was. He would have been well-known because "all nations shall call you blessed." You see, no matter which way you take it, tithing is a starting point. You start there and all kinds of things come together for you. If you don't, all kinds of things start to fall apart. You want to be something in the mind of the community, you start with tithing. You want to be blessed in your land, that area that you make your living in, you start with tithing. God will elevate your reputation. I mean it starts here.

God doesn't have you until He gets your pocketbook. Because when He has your pocketbook, He has you. He wants your heart first because if He doesn't have that He knows He won't have that pocketbook either. So it all starts right here with tithing.

There are seven distinct blessings associated with tithing. They are broad in their sweep and long lasting in their effect. You must see this thing from the viewpoint of God. You must see it like Abraham saw it. It is a blessing pack. It was not a command to Abraham. He did it because it was right. And look what the man got back. There was no law that made him do it. He just did it because it should have been done, and he wound up probably the richest man of his day.

There's where it starts, with the tithe. It's not that we have to tithe. It is that we get to. And look at all the seven blessings that follow with it.

Chapter Three

The Second Step You Must Take To Claim Abrahamic Blessings

We preach many evangelistic sermons from Galatians 6:7-10. And it is legitimate. But, actually, we take it out of context when we do it because this scripture has a totally different meaning within the context here. I want to share it with you and show you some things from it that will build your faith and bless you greatly.

> **Gal 6:7-10**
> **7 Be not deceived; God is not mocked: for whatsoever a man soweth, that shall he also reap.**
> **8 For he that soweth to his flesh shall of the flesh reap corruption; but he that soweth to the Spirit shall of the Spirit reap life everlasting.**
> **9 And let us not be weary in well doing: for in due season we shall reap, if we faint not.**
> **10 As we have therefore opportunity, let us do good unto all men, especially unto them who are of the household of faith. (KJV)**

We usually preach a man right to the edge of hell with this passage. But this is taking it out of its context, because in this context it is speaking to Christians concerning what they can expect by way of reaping contingent upon what they sow. "For he that soweth to his flesh, shall of the flesh reap corruption. He that soweth to the Spirit, shall the Spirit reap life everlasting."

But verse 9 is the real heart of this passage. "Let us not be weary in well doing: for in due season, we shall reap if we faint not. As we, therefore, have opportunity let us do good unto all men especially unto them who are of the household of faith." Now, where Paul is coming from in this letter to the Galatians is this: These people need to take advantage of opportunities to do good to other people. Why? Because in "well doing" for other people, God is not mocked.

In other words, you don't need to think you are going to make a mockery out of God and His Laws that He has set into place in His universe. God is not going to be made a fool of concerning the laws that He has set into place in His universe. Therefore, you don't need to be deceived into thinking God can be made a fool of, or mocked, in that some guy out there can either change one of God's laws or violate one of God's laws and get away with it.

It's like a fellow getting on top of a building and jumping off, and thinking he is going to defy gravity and go up instead of down. That guy has deceived himself if he thinks that is going to happen. God and His law would have to be mocked. To say that somebody can reverse His process and make His law work differently from the way God set it up is literally to mock God. But God is not mocked!

Now this context speaks of sowing and reaping which is God's universal law just like gravity is God's universal law. And like gravity, God's law of sowing and reaping continues to function unless God Himself intervenes in that law, offsets it and forces it to work some other way. It is set in concrete. Be not deceived. God is not mocked. Whatever a man soweth, that shall that same man also reap because this is how God has set up and established this law. Now, He says here, "let us not be weary in well doing."

Sometimes we are called upon to do things for other people when we don't feel like doing it. It just wearies us to have to do it. I have this dear person that calls me for prayer. This person is subject to call anytime of the day or night and does. Now I have never met this individual. But, she has my name and my number. And she calls whenever "the spirit moves" on her which may be at 3:00 o'clock in the morning. I can tell you her name. I know her voice. She has some of the wildest prayer requests I have ever heard in my life. Well, what am I going to do about this? I can get rid of her in a flash.

But you see, if I get weary in well doing, (the law of sowing and reaping works continuously whether I think it does or not), then the reaping is going to suffer also. Do you see? So I have never hung up on this person. I have never put the phone down. I have never been rude. I do discourage her taking thirty minutes to tell me what her problem is. I sort of say, just get to the point, and she will get to the point. And I say, "Ma'am, I will pray for you." Then she says thank you and goes on her way. So, it's over within two minutes. Then I pray for her. I am not going to be weary in well doing concerning this lady.

Now, let us not be weary in well doing. Why? For in due season we shall reap, if we faint not. This is God's universal law which you cannot make a mockery of. Whatever you sow is actually what you are going to reap. That statement is in concrete and any attempt to change it is to make a mockery of God, and you are not going to do that.

Does anyone reading these lines honestly think that you can actually make a fool of God? Are you that audacious? I am not. I have learned that if there is anybody that is going to be made a fool of it's me. It's not going to be God that is made a fool of. So in due season we shall reap if we faint not.

I want you to see another important truth in this scripture: *there is a season.* There is a season for reaping. There is a season for planting and cultivating. But there is a season for reaping. Now I don't need to expect to reap prior to the season. I also don't need to expect to reap if I have not sown first. I also don't need to expect to reap a harvest in the reaping season if I have not cultivated in the cultivating season what I have sown in the sowing season. There is a season of reaping provided we faint not.

Did you grow up on a farm? I did. There's a season for all of this. Now there will be no season for reaping if you don't sow. There will be no season for reaping if you don't cultivate. But if you do these two in their proper seasons, there is going to be a reaping. The average little Christianette today doesn't understand this sowing and cultivating part, He just wants to reap. He wants something for nothing. Not even God can produce a harvest where there has been no seed sown. He can, but He won't. Therefore, He can't. So, you better get these ducks lined up and get the sowing and the cultivating done first, so that the season for the reaping can come in its due course.

God said for us not be weary in well doing because in due season we shall reap, if we faint not. And then He says for us, as we have the opportunity, to do good unto all men, especially unto them who are of the household of faith. Why should I do good? Because I am sowing and I am going to get back a harvest of the same thing I sowed. If I sow good I am going to reap good. Sowing and reaping is what the context of this scripture is about. So what we need to do is concentrate on the doing of good.

One of the greatest, spiritual lessons I ever learned was in front of a grocery store just a short number of years ago. I pulled up in my car to get out and go in that store to get something. There was a fellow there who was dirty, sitting on the sidewalk at the front of this store. When I went in, the guy asked me to give him some money because he was hungry. He was homeless and he had no work. He couldn't find any work. He wanted me to buy him a sandwich. I thought he is nothing but a wino bum and I am not about to give him a penny because when I am gone he will go buy wine.

I have been like that all my life. I just wouldn't give them the time of day. I had the attitude people like that were just bums. If there was anything to them, they would get off that joy-juice and get out there and make something of themselves and quit this bumming around. So I told him no I didn't have anything for him. By the time I got inside the door the Holy Ghost hit me like a ton of bricks over that situation. I sort of put it off and went about my business in the store. When I came out, I could see the guy going down the side-walk. As I went to my car God was still doing a number on me. He said, "You catch that man and you give him some money." And I am saying, "Lord he is a bum. He is a wino. You know what he will do with this." And the Lord said, "You give him some money." So I gave in to the voice of God.

I went down the sidewalk and got the man's attention. I didn't have that much money in my pocket, $10, maybe. Anyway, I took the money out and gave it to him. The man looked at me so startled. Furthermore, I have never been blessed so much in my life as I was when I gave him that money. Why? Because the Bible says "from him that asketh of thee, turn not thou away," period.

I am not responsible for what he does with it. I am not responsible that he is a wino or is not a wino. But I am responsible to respond to a man in need. That was the turning around point in my life. Because good has come my way ever since.

As we, therefore, have opportunity let us do good unto all men, especially them who are of the household of faith. I don't know if that man was of the household of faith or not, but this much I know. I did good to a man. I responded and I obeyed. Now, people come in my church all the time, and they need gas money or they need this or they need that and no questions asked, I'll reach in my pocket and pull out what little money I have and give it to them. I know that I will never see them again. They say "I will send it to you in the mail." I know it is a lie. They never will. But that doesn't bother me. Why? Because I am sowing, and good is coming back because I am doing good. You see, I am sowing. There is a time to sow. There is a time to reap. I have built up a backlog, so now I reap all the time.

This is how it works. Be not deceived, you are not going to make a mockery out of God and change the rules. Learn what the rules are and play by them. Just start giving and doing good and watching God bring it back. That's simple to understand. Even I can figure that out and understand it. It is just a matter of walking it out.

Now go to Luke 6:38. This is everybody's favorite verse. We are not talking about tithing now. Tithing is the starting point. We are talking to the graduating class here. I mean, you go beyond tithing and you give an offering. That's when it all really starts to pop, brother. Things start to happen. Do you doubt God? Then, you need to start doing what we are talking about in these pages and see what comes into your life.

> **Luke 6:38**
> **38 Give, and it shall be given unto you; good measure, pressed down, and shaken together, and running over, shall men give into your bosom. For with the same measure that ye mete withal it shall be measured to you again.**
> **(KJV)**

Notice what Jesus said. He said "Give and it shall be given unto you." He said "it" shall be given unto you. What is "it"? "It" is a pronoun which is the noun that "it" represents in this sentence. Well, "it" is whatever you give. **Whatever you give.** If you need a big harvest, you need to sow a big seed because "it" shall be given unto you. If your "it" is big, your harvest will be big also. You determine the size of your harvest by the size of your "it."

I asked before, if you were raised on a farm. I was. When I was a little boy my dad started teaching me responsibility. One time he gave me some seed. He wanted me to plant a row and he told me how far apart to plant the seeds. He was going to come back with a plow and cover them up. This was before the days of automatic machinery. So I planted a little way down that row like he asked me to do. But that was a big bucket of seed and that was one long row for a little boy. I thought, "I never will get through with this row." I had only planted about ten seeds; so I took that whole bucket of seed and put it very thickly in a space of just a few feet. Then, I went down that row and sort of covered that few feet over with my foot. You know, I put that whole bucket of seed in just a few feet of space, but none of the balance of that row had any seed in it. Well, I had covered it over where my dad wouldn't see it. When he came down there he covered up what he thought was a row that had been completely planted.

When the field started coming up, there wasn't enough ground to hold the stuff coming out of the short space that I had sowed. But the rest of the row was blank. Nothing came up on it. Well, my dad knew immediately what I had done. You see, give and it shall be given back to you. I sowed thickly in a matter of a few feet, and brother, I reaped thickly in a matter of a few feet, but reaped nothing down the balance of the row.

A lot of Christians have that great speckled bird syndrome. They want to come down the aisle, put their monthly dollar in the plate, go outside and look up in the sky and see that great speckled bird come sailing over and drop fifty pounds of gold pieces right in their lap. It doesn't work like that. You see, you haven't sown properly in order to reap a bag full of fifty dollar gold pieces. Start sowing like that and you *will* reap like that.

But if you sow a dollar here and a dollar there, a dollar here and a dollar there is all you will ever reap. If dollar sowing is all you are capable of at this point, God will bless it and multiply it back to you so you can graduate into sowing greater. If you are capable of sowing greater than a dollar now and yet you do only dollar sowing, that's robbing God in the process. Your reaping is going to be as meager as your sowing. Because you sowed just a small amount of seed, you are going to reap a small amount from it.

Give and it shall be given unto you. Whatever you give is what God is going to take as raw material to give back to you. "It" is a pronoun which replaces a noun in the sentence. Well, there is no noun here. It is implied. And the implied noun is "whatever you sow," and whatever you sow determines the magnitude, quality, and quantity of your harvest.

Now notice something else. Whatever you give, even if it is meager, God does some things to it. He gives it back. But, He gives back more than you gave. When He gives it back, it's good measure, and it's pressed down, and it's shaken together. Did you ever go in the grocery store and buy a tall box of cereal and you get home and open it up, and the box is not full? Did you ever do that? Sure you have. Or potato chips. That's what really upsets me - to get a big, puffy bag of fresh potato chips (they know how to puff those bags up), and you get home and it's settled and there's not a full bag. That's why they

46

show the weight on the package. (They measure it by weight and not by space.) I want it by space. That's why I buy that big bag.

But anyway, it's not like that when God does business with you. It's not like the cereal boxes. I mean, that thing shrinks for some reason. But notice God takes what you give and gives it back, but He does it good measure, pressed down, shaken together, and running over. Now the cereal box is good measure, pressed down, shaken together; but brother, it is not running over. God makes it run out and over the top.

Now these are the laws by which God works. You see, God wants to do good to his people. I spent so many years in the ministry thinking God was gleefully flying around the sky trying to catch me in something, so He could zap me and hurt me. I gave Him plenty to zap me over, because I needed more help than most. Can you identify with me? I read this philosopher, William James, who wrote a book, Varieties of Religious Experience. He made a statement that was just profound. He said some people are just holier than others. And I thought, "Yea, and I am one of them that's not." I mean I have to work at it. He said some people just seem to have a born disposition to be up to their neck at all times. I said "that one up to his neck is me." So I had this view that God was just continuously keeping score on me, to do me up and get me. And I found out that is not the case. God is in the business of blessing His people.

I found out that God really likes a guy like me. Why? Because I make a lot of mistakes, but I get a lot done too. That's one thing about it, when my time is up I'm not going to rust out. I may burn out, but I am not rusting out. A guy like that will make a lot of mistakes, but he will also get a lot done. So you see, God likes even people like me. If you are like I am, making a lot of mistakes, God likes you. He loves us. He wants to help us. When you begin to play it His way and give, He has laws that take effect. Those laws mean this: He will shake it down, press it together, make it good measure, and run it out the top so that you have an overflow and an abundance of what you invested by your giving to start with.

Then He says how He is going to do it. "Shall men give into your bosom." He is going to make men give to me, running over, what I gave Him. Let me illustrate this by an experience my wife and I had when we were getting set to go off to preaching school. In our denomination, at that time, you had to go to preaching school. (They think you can't preach if you don't go to preaching school.) So we were getting set to go to preaching school. My wife's mother was a member of a little independent church out on the north side of Houston, pastored by a converted Jew, named Solomon Davis, a saintly, godly man. Well, my wife and I were there that night. It was our last night in Houston. We were going to Marshall, Texas to go to preaching school. Now, I had put off going to preaching school for two years, because I never could get the money. So I finally said, "Lord, if you want me to go, you are going to have to work this out, because I have just been unable to get ahead. So I am just going to have to shut everything down and go, and You are going to have to provide for me; otherwise, I just won't be able to do it." So by faith, I quit my job, got set to go, and we went to that church our last night there.

I still didn't have any money. I was just going. I did, however, have $55 in my pocket. I had a car that had a payment due and the payment was $55. I had to go across Texas, from Houston to Marshall, with $55, and I owed that. I had to get a place to live when I got there. I had to buy gas. I had to feed a wife, and wives love to eat. I had to pay tuition and buy books on fifty-five bucks and I owed that on my car alone.

While sitting there during the song service, it dawned on me I hadn't paid tithes on the last pay check I received. I owed $7 out of that $55. I thought, "Lord, I am going in the hole by the minute here. I shouldn't have come." That was the longest song service I believe I ever experienced in my life. While they sang their "200,000 songs," I became the centerpiece in a tug-of-war. The devil was on one side and God was on the other, and I and that $7 were up for grabs in the middle. I am serious. It is funny now, but it wasn't funny that night because, back then, $7 was a bunch of bucks; it was a lot of money. So, I was sitting there and they sang and sang and sang and sang and the devil played games with me big time. He would point to their Sunday School board up at the front. They put their Sunday School attendance up on a board where everyone could see it. They also put the amount of the Sunday morning offering up on the board. Meanwhile, the devil was telling me, look up there. Look how many they had in Sunday School this morning. Look at the size of that offering. They don't need your $7.

I said to him, "You are right. Yea, you are right." And he said, "Besides that, you are going to be out serving God, aren't you?" I said, "Yea." He said, "That 7 bucks is God's money, isn't it?" I said, "Yea." He said, "Well just pay yourself your first paycheck." I said, "I think I will." He was doing a real number on me. I don't know if the devil plays games with you, but he plays them with me. Consequently, here I was sitting in church agreeing with him on the one hand, and feeling the Holy Ghost tugging at me about $7 tithe on the other hand. I was in a tug-of-war for real.

Finally, the moment of truth came. They passed that plate down the aisle where I was sitting and when it came to me, I just held on to it. I looked at it and held it and looked at it and held it and looked at it.

49

Finally, everybody else was looking to see who had the offering plate, and I was sitting there just holding it and staring at it. The moment of truth had come, dear brother and sister. What do I do with my $7 that I needed so much? Well, I reached in my pocket and got my $7 and put it in that plate and watched it as it went down the row and disappeared out of my life. Now, you think that wasn't tough? That was a bridge for me to cross. I was just starting out in my Christian life and as a new Christian, I never had the benefit of a pastor, never did. Right after I got saved, my pastor left our church. I never, as a saved man, had a pastor. Never. I had to hack it out by myself. So I had nobody to talk to about this. Furthermore, the devil's arguments were making sense with me because I needed this money. You see, I was not going out to the beer joint to spend $7. I was going off to "learn to preach." I was going to be serving God. And God had said, "Put it in the plate." So I did. I let it go and I watched it. I thought I would die.

There were only a handful of people there that night and when the service was over Brother Davis said, "I want ya'll to come by and shake hands with Jay. He is going off to school." So they did. They shook hands with me and they put money, both coins and paper, in my hand. I put it in my pocket. My wife and I went to our car, that we owed that $55 payment on, turned on the light and before we ever left the parking lot, counted it. There was just a couple of one dollar bills and everything else was change, because there were mostly little children there that night. Do you know how much money it was? $7. You can't beat God. You cannot make a mockery of God, His Word or His laws. What did He say? "Give and it shall be given unto you," and I just proved it. "Give and it shall be given unto you, and He will cause men to give it into your bosom." Now that was a moment of truth for me. I kid you not. I watched that plate go down the end of the row with my money in it. Have any of you ever been in a situation like that?

We have to learn to trust God, and this is not always easy. Sometimes God will bring you face-to-face with the reality of what His Word says in one area and force you to either accept it or reject it. If you accept it, He will force you to literally step out on it. And that gets spooky, especially the first few times you do it. Anybody identify with me in this? Understand something here, dear reader. We rarely ever are called upon to step out on everything in God's Word at once. Our human frame and system are incapable of that. But God will engineer events and circumstances where He brings you face-to-face with one issue covered by His Word and force you to walk out on it or fold up your tent. If you fold up, He will re-engineer the circumstances and bring you right back to face it again. So you might as well move out on it. The area covered in this book is giving. He says, "Give and it shall be given unto you." Now, look at Proverbs 11:24.

> **Prov 11:24-26**
> **24 There is that scattereth, and yet increaseth; and there is**
> **that withholdeth more than is meet, but it tendeth to poverty.**
> **25 The liberal soul shall be made fat; and he that watereth**
> **shall be watered also himself.**
> **26 He that withholdeth corn, the people shall curse him; but**
> **blessing shall be upon the head of him that selleth it. (KJV)**

"There is he that scatterth and yet increaseth." Now, how can I increase something if I am just scattering it out? But it works like that. This is God's way. By giving, I get. Look at what He says. "There is he that scatterth yet increaseth and there is he that withholdeth more than is fitting for him to hold, but that tendeth to poverty." God's system of economics is totally different from the world's. The world says if you want to get ahead, save X number of dollars out of your paycheck, invest it in bank CD's for a certain amount of interest rates, and so forth and so on. And that's how you get ahead. Well, that's true up to a point, but God's system goes beyond that and says if you want to get ahead, scatter. Because if you save everything, according to God's system, this "tendeth to poverty."

Now, when you have something from God, let's call it "seed." There are three things you can do with your seed.

*You can eat your seed.
*You can save your seed until it rots and dies.
*You can plant your seed.

The seed must be planted. The great mistake is when we eat our seed. Suppose a man makes some extra money and blows every dime of it. That is eating the seed. Or he gets some extra money and runs down and sticks it in the bank account for 3 1/2% interest. That's saving all the seed. Now, the best and smartest thing would be to take some of that seed and plant it, so that the seed would bring back more harvest. If you eat everything that you get, don't look for a harvest next year. You are going to be on the street looking for a job. So there is the guy that scatters, but that guy increases.

If the seed is not planted, it's not working. It's not in the ground. It's not doing anything. It is just out there dead. Whether you eat it or you save it makes no difference. One way or the other it's not circulating. So the third option is to scatter. There's he that scatterth, yet he increases. And then there is the man that puts it in the can and sits on it and that tends to poverty.

The liberal soul shall be made fat in verse 25. He that watereth shall be watered also himself, because he is scattering. He is liberally scattering. I liberally sowed seed in that four or five feet in the row my dad gave me responsibility over. Well, I was liberal there and I got back a liberal harvest right there. The rest of that row didn't produce anything because I didn't put anything into it. The Bible says "he that watereth shall be watered also himself." And "He that withholdeth," verse 26, "the people shall curse him: but blessings shall be upon the head of him that selleth it."

Now what are you going to do here? Everybody says they don't have any extra money and can't afford to tithe, give an offering and or engage in the first fruit ceremonies. Well, do you have cable TV? You have an extra 18 bucks a month. I had it put in my house so that I could get the Disney channel for my granddaughters and TBN for my wife and me. I told the cable company I didn't want HBO and Showtime and Cinemax. I don't want to clutter up my brain with what I see on TV. When I get up to preach, I want my mind to be as pure as I can get it. If I have filth piped into my home the night before, via TV, my mind is not pure. So I told them I didn't want it. Well, they hooked it up anyway. I was not paying for it. But that is their way to get you hooked, so they can come back to you a month later and threaten to cut it off. But by then you will say, "No, I decided I can afford these programs. Don't cut them off." You see, you have gotten used to that filth. Well, they left that stuff in my home two months. So I had my wife call them up and say, "Hey, come get this stuff out of here or you come take this whole cable out, I don't want on it at all." Well, to say the least, they came and took it out. My point is this: I put Disney in there for my granddaughters, but you know, I can get along even without that.

There must be some scattering seed left in my bank account just as there must be in your bank account. There just has to be because somewhere you are going to need a harvest. That harvest comes, not based on the fact that you need it, but it comes based upon the fact that you sowed seed for it. Now if you haven't sowed seed for it, I don't care how great your need is, you are not going to have a harvest. God Almighty is not obligated to give you one until you sow some of what He has given you to start with. To get set for a rainy day, you must start sowing now. God is not obligated to come through for you, if you have been eating all the seed He has given you down through the years. What we need to do is this: start sowing some of the seed we have been eating so that we can reap a harvest when the season of harvest comes for us.

This is how it works. This is God's system, and God is not mocked. You are not going to make a fool of God by changing up the rules. This is set in concrete. You sow, you reap. You give, men will give back into your bosom. There is a man that scattereth yet increases. Now this is God's Word, people. It is His System. This system keeps a man humble because it makes him recognize his absolute, total dependence on God.

The world's universities teach about an economic system that functions differently. They set it up where they can do it their way, where they honestly think they don't need God. But, when you and I do it God's Way, we don't have to hustle like they do.

You know where I am in scripture? I am over there in the book of Hebrew where it talks about "rest" for the people of God. I am at perfect rest. I don't get bent out of shape about anything. I am totally at rest. I am at peace. I am at rest and if I need something, I sow something and I get it in the harvest.

So, your second step to Abrahamic blessings is to give offerings in addition to your tithe.

Father, bless us now as we concentrate on these things. Lord, build the faith of your children. Increase us. Increase our borders. In Jesus Name. Amen.

Chapter Four

The Third Step You Must Take
To Claim Abrahamic Blessings

You will benefit greatly if you will read the following scripture passage through at least three times and meditate deeply in it prior to reading the balance of this chapter.

Deut 26:1-19
1 And it shall be, when thou art come in unto the land which the LORD thy God giveth thee for an inheritance, and possessest it, and dwellest therein;
2 That thou shalt take of the first of all the fruit of the earth, which thou shalt bring of thy land that the LORD thy God giveth thee, and shalt put it in a basket, and shalt go unto the place which the LORD thy God shall choose to place his name there.
3 And thou shalt go unto the priest that shall be in those days, and say unto him, I profess this day unto the LORD thy God, that I am come unto the country which the LORD sware unto our fathers for to give us.
4 And the priest shall take the basket out of thine hand, and set it down before the altar of the LORD thy God.
5 And thou shalt speak and say before the LORD thy God, A Syrian ready to perish was my father, and he went down into Egypt, and sojourned there with a few, and became there a nation, great, mighty, and populous:
6 And the Egyptians evil entreated us, and afflicted us, and laid upon us hard bondage:
7 And when we cried unto the LORD God of our fathers, the LORD heard our voice, and looked on our affliction, and our labour, and our oppression:
8 And the LORD brought us forth out of Egypt with a mighty hand, and with an outstretched arm, and with great terribleness,

and with signs, and with wonders:

9 And he hath brought us into this place, and hath given us this land, even a land that floweth with milk and honey.

10 And now, behold, I have brought the firstfruits of the land, which thou, O LORD, hast given me. And thou shalt set it before the LORD thy God, and worship before the LORD thy God:

11 And thou shalt rejoice in every good thing which the LORD thy God hath given unto thee, and unto thine house, thou, and the Levite, and the stranger that is among you.

12 When thou hast made an end of tithing all the tithes of thine increase the third year, which is the year of tithing, and hast given it unto the Levite, the stranger, the fatherless, and the widow, that they may eat within thy gates, and be filled;

13 Then thou shalt say before the LORD thy God, I have brought away the hallowed things out of mine house, and also have given them unto the Levite, and unto the stranger, to the fatherless, and to the widow, according to all thy commandments which thou hast commanded me: I have not transgressed thy commandments, neither have I forgotten them:

14 I have not eaten thereof in my mourning, neither have I taken away ought thereof for any unclean use, nor given ought thereof for the dead: but I have hearkened to the voice of the LORD my God, and have done according to all that thou hast commanded me.

15 Look down from thy holy habitation, from heaven, and bless thy people Israel, and the land which thou hast given us, as thou swarest unto our fathers, a land that floweth with milk and honey.

16 This day the LORD thy God hath commanded thee to do these statutes and judgments: thou shalt therefore keep and do them with all thine heart, and with all thy soul.

17 Thou hast avouched the LORD this day to be thy God, and to walk in his ways, and to keep his statutes, and his commandments, and his judgments, and to hearken unto his voice:

18 And the LORD hath avouched thee this day to be his peculiar people, as he hath promised thee, and that thou shouldest keep all his commandments;

19 And to make thee high above all nations which he hath made, in praise, and in name, and in honour; and that thou mayest

be an holy people unto the LORD thy God, as he hath spoken. (KJV)

There were three national feasts in the life of Israel. One of these feasts was the feast of The First Fruits which operated by a law, the law of the offering of the first fruits. Now, we have to remember that Israel in the Old Testament was the Abrahamic Seed Group. We have to remember that most of what was said to them, concerning them, applies to us today because you and I, Gentile Christians, are now members of the Abraham Seed Group, right along with them. So those things in the Old Testament that have not been changed by Jesus Christ, are valid and applicable to and for us today. We have been grafted into the same identical Abrahamic system because the church today is the Abrahamic system of the Old Testament with Gentiles grafted in.

As such, there are some blessings promised concerning the first fruits for the Abrahamic Seed Group. We are going to take a look at the law of the offering of the First Fruits here.

> **Deut 26:1-3**
> **1 And it shall be, when thou art come in unto the land which the LORD thy God giveth thee for an inheritance, and possessest it, and dwellest therein;**
> **2 That thou shalt take of the first of all the fruit of the earth, which thou shalt bring of thy land that the LORD thy God giveth thee, and shalt put it in a basket, and shalt go unto the place which the LORD thy God shall choose to place his name there.**
> **3 And thou shalt go unto the priest that shall be in those days, and say unto him, I profess this day unto the LORD thy God, that I am come unto the country which the LORD sware unto our fathers for to give us. (KJV)**

I am going to point out eight things from these scriptures that the members of *The Abrahamic Seed Group* are to do with their first fruits. The first fruits, for you, has to do with the first thing that you get from your labors. Whether you get it from your land, whether you get if from your job, whether you get it from somebody giving it to you, is immaterial. But it is the first fruits of that which comes into your possession.

First, "thou shalt take it and put it in a basket." The first thing you do, then, is take the first fruit and put in a basket. That is what He says here. "Thou shalt take it and put it in a basket."

Second, "thou shalt go unto the place which the LORD thy God shall choose to place His Name there."

Third, "thou shalt go unto the priest who shall be in those days."

Fourth, "thou shalt say some things unto the priest."

Here are the four things we have in this passage. Take your first fruits and put them in a basket. That basket can be your purse, your check-book, your billfold, the trunk of your car. It could be the biggest CD that has ever been written by your bank. But if it is the first fruits, put it in a basket or however you want to carry it. The basket is a carrying container. Go to the place where God is pleased to put His Name. Third, go to the priest. And fourth, make a profession unto him and say, "I profess this day unto the Lord thy God that I am come unto the country which the Lord swore unto our fathers to give us." That confession is an acknowledgment with your lips to the man of God that what you have is not because of you, but because of what God gave you.

Deuteronomy 8:18 reminds us we are to remember that it is the Lord that gave us the power to get wealth, lest when we get it, we are prone to say, "Well, I did that. I did that with my own abilities. I did that with my wits." Now that's wrong. We are to remember that it is God that gave us the power to get wealth.

We bring the first fruits in our basket to the place where God chooses to place His Name, bring it to the priest, and say to the priest, "I profess to God that this is the first fruits of what He has given me." We are acknowledging two things to the man of God. First, here is the offering of my first fruits. Second, God is responsible for me having it to start with. So we put it in a basket, we take it to the place, we go to the priest, and we "profess" to the priest. Next, we see what the priest does with it.

> **Deut 26:4**
> **4 And the priest shall take the basket out of thine hand, and set it down before the altar of the LORD thy God. (KJV)**

Now, are you beginning to see that something is wrong with the way we receive an offering in so many of our churches? We sort of short-circuit and shortcut. This first fruits offering should be brought in a basket, and given to the priest. The pastor-priest is an interchangeable term. The pastor-priest shall set it down before the altar of the Lord thy God. Then the pastor-priest is through temporarily.

Then, in verses 5 through 10, the one that brings the first fruits offering is given another set of instructions. "Thou shalt speak and say before the Lord thy God." There are several verses listed here which show what a physical descendent of Abraham was supposed to "speak and say." I want to show you these verses and then apply them to us today. We are not physical Jews. Therefore, I believe that our confession here is going to be a little different, but I want you to see exactly *what* they "professed." Then, I want you to catch the *spirit* of what they "professed."

Keep in mind these are Jews that are making this confession. They "say" their father was a Syrian, verse 5, who was ready to perish.

> **Deut 26:5**
> **5 And thou shalt speak and say before the LORD thy God, A Syrian ready to perish was my father, and he went down into Egypt, and sojourned there with a few, and became there a nation, great, mighty, and populous: (KJV)**

Now, how can a Jew's father be a Syrian and not a Jew? Because Abraham was a Gentile, remember? Prior to Abraham there was no Jew, no Hebrew, no Israeli. They were all heathen Gentiles. So Abraham was a Syrian. They became the chosen race through Abraham. But prior to that, there was no chosen race. Everybody was as heathen as you can get, including Abraham. Not one thing about him recommended him to God. He was as big an idolater as ever lived. But God in His grace reached down, singled him out, and made the covenant with him.

But there was nothing in Abraham that made him deserve God's grace. There was nothing good in him that made God say, "I'll do business with him." There was nothing in Abraham that made God think that. He was a Syrian. He was a heathen. He was an idolater. So this was something that a Jew had a difficult time acknowledging; his father, his ancestor, was a Syrian. That is humbling. So the *spirit* of this confession is *humility*. Next, look at *what* they confessed.

> **Deut 26:6-10**
> **6 And the Egyptians evil entreated us, and afflicted us, and laid upon us hard bondage:**
> **7 And when we cried unto the LORD God of our fathers, the**

LORD heard our voice, and looked on our affliction, and our labour, and our oppression:
8 And the LORD brought us forth out of Egypt with a mighty hand, and with an outstretched arm, and with great terribleness, and with signs, and with wonders:
9 And he hath brought us into this place, and hath given us this land, even a land that floweth with milk and honey.
10 And now, behold, I have brought the first fruits of the land, which thou, O LORD, hast given me. And thou shalt set it before the LORD thy God, and worship before the LORD thy God: (KJV)

What is in the above confession? It retraces the *history* of The Abrahamic Seed Group from the time of Abraham throughout their Egyptian captivity. It retraces the fact that God delivered them from that captivity and gave them the promised land.

But what is there in it that you and I can use as a pattern for ourselves? First, there is humility. They had to confess that, although they were Jews, they had a Syrian father, Abraham. Second, they acknowledged that everything they had came from the hand of God. They were slaves and God delivered them. Yet God delivered those people just like He delivered the slaves from that ungodliness in this country. They recognized the fact that God was their source. Humiliation, coupled with the fact that God was their source, was their confession. Not what I did...not how smart I am...not how great my talents are...not what breaks I had...not the network of people that I know, but God was the source. They recognized it and professed it. That's what's in that confession.

Let's go on. When the confession is over, instructions start again. The sixth thing they were to do was this: "Thou shalt set it before the Lord thy God."

> **10 ...And thou shalt set it before the LORD thy God, and worship before the LORD thy God: (KJV)**

They brought it to the priest who set it down before the altar of the Lord thy God. When our confession is over *we* are to set it before the Lord. The priest sets it before the altar of the Lord, but once the confession is made, we are to "set it" before the Lord ourselves.

This says to me, again, the way we usually receive an offering just won't get it. It's too casual. It is too nonchalant. It's just too much form. It's too easy. There's not that setting before the Lord of the first fruit. Yet that is part of the instructions. "Thou shalt set it," verse 10, "before the Lord thy God."

The seventh thing they were instructed to do in the offering of the First Fruits was this: "thou shalt worship before the Lord thy God." As you "say and speak" your profession, and as you "set it," you worship. You worship in that you acknowledge God as the source of it. You worship in that you "set it" there literally to give the first fruits to God.

And then, number 8, "thou shalt rejoice in every good thing which the Lord thy God has given unto thee and unto thine house, thou, and the Levite, and the stranger who is among you," verse 11.

Deut 26:11
11 And thou shalt rejoice in every good thing which the LORD thy God hath given unto thee, and unto thine house, thou, and the Levite, and the stranger that is among you. (KJV)

We have eight distinct instructions here about the first fruits. Let's review them. First, put it in a basket. Second, go to the place with that basket where the Lord chooses to place His name. Third, go to the priest whoever he may be and make a confession unto that man of God saying, "I profess this day unto the Lord thy God that I am come unto the country which the Lord swore unto our fathers to give us."

I think I need to add another bit of instruction here. Do you see the expression, "which the Lord swore unto our fathers to give us"? "Our fathers" always, in Scripture, means Abraham, Isaac, and Jacob. Anytime that you see that expression, it always includes them because everything traces back to Abraham. God promised land in the Abrahamic Covenant to the physical descendants of Abraham.

So they always give credit to that covenant and God's promise in that covenant to Abraham. Learn to think in terms of the Abrahamic Covenant, because there is no blessing, no salvation, no healing, no prosperity, there's no nothing for you as a Christian apart from the Abrahamic Covenant. It all goes back to Abraham. Consequently, he acknowledges and confesses that all these things are because God promised it to him in the Abrahamic Covenant through the fathers.

Then the fourth thing is the priest has to set it before the altar of the Lord. But, number 5, we "speak and say" before the Lord our God giving Him our background and history. We praise the Lord for all the things that Jesus has brought us through. You see, this was simply rehearsing in their mind and with their lips the things that God brought them through as the physical descendants of Abraham, as God was taking them out of slavery in Egypt and bringing them into the land that God promised in the Abrahamic Covenant. So they began to tell God about it. They just confessed their history. We need to do that.

Every day of my life, I can think of something that God miraculously delivered me from. I am a man that should never preach again because the devil has done as much to shut my mouth and stop my ministry as any man I know in modern America. But here I am by the glory and the grace of God. Neither man nor devil can ever shut my mouth. It just can't be done because God is in control of me and responsible for me. He has called me into the ministry and nobody is going to shut that up. So I can just go back and think about all the things that have happened to me, that people have done to me to wipe me out and put me out of the ministry and shut my mouth. But, here I am still preaching. However, most of those who tried to silence me have been silenced themselves, long ago. People that have tried to put me out of business are now out of business themselves. But not me. Why? Because I keep on preaching by the grace of God. Go back and tell God about your history. Thank Him for it. Confess it. The confession goes with the first fruits offering. You are recognizing and acknowledging with your profession, combined with your first fruits offering, that God is the Source of everything you have. God not only gives, He also sustains. So we tell Him about it in our history. Then, when we tell Him that we brought the first fruits in verse 10, we actually set the thing before the Lord. We set it.

From what we have seen above, it appears to me that we need to change the way we receive the offerings in many of our churches. We set that offering before the Lord. That's what it says. We set it before the Lord. Thou shalt set it before the Lord thy God and not only that, we shall rejoice in every good thing which the Lord thy God has given thee. Now I have a lot to rejoice about. I am tall and slender, but I am not hungry. I have a shirt, a car, a house, and I'm healthy. You see, we have a lot to rejoice about.

If the church took care of their stewardship financially we wouldn't need the government messing around with the welfare program. We would and could do it better. Now a lot of churches may not, but I believe that most of them would. Bless God, we would do it because we would be able to do it. And we would do it better than the government ever will be able to do it. If the first fruits were offered by everybody, we would be in the welfare business because the church has no business accumulating riches. Their money is supposed to be used in ministering.

Go to verses 13 and 14. There are more instructions here concerning things that we are supposed to say next.

> **Deut 26:13-14**
> **13 Then thou shalt say before the LORD thy God, I have brought away the hallowed things out of mine house, and also have given them unto the Levite, and unto the stranger, to the fatherless, and to the widow, according to all thy commandments which thou hast commanded me: I have not transgressed thy commandments, neither have I forgotten them:**
> **14 I have not eaten thereof in my mourning, neither have I taken away ought thereof for any unclean use, nor given ought thereof for the dead: but I have hearkened to the voice of the LORD my God, and have done according to all that thou hast commanded me. (KJV)**

We are to say these things.
1. I have brought my hallowed things.
2. I have given them to people that need it.
3. I have not transgressed thy commandments.
4. Neither have I forgotten them.
5. I have not eaten thereof in my mourning.
6. Neither have I taken away anything thereof for any unclean use.
7. Neither have I given anything thereof for the dead.
8. I have harkened to the voice of the Lord my God.
9. I have done according to all that Thou has commanded me.

These are the things we are to "say before the Lord thy God" as we bring the first fruits and give it all to God. This kind of giving coupled with this kind of confession will get the Mind, and Heart, and Ear of our Father God in a flash.

Next, in verse 15, we are in a position to ask something. Based on all the above, the person making his first fruits offering says:

> **Deut 26:15**
> **15 Look down from thy holy habitation, from heaven, and bless thy people Israel, and the land which thou hast given us, as thou swearest unto our fathers, a land that floweth with milk and honey. (KJV)**

Dear reader, if I honor God like that, I am entitled to ask God to help me and to bless me. I am also entitled to expect God to do it because He promised in the Abrahamic Covenant that He would do it. This is what the Bible says about the first fruits.

The offering of The First Fruits was so important in the mind of God that He made it a national religious event that they were to do. The First Fruit offering was to be taken up at the beginning of the harvest. When the harvest began, they brought the first fruits and gave them to God. They were mostly agricultural, and they made their offering at the time of harvest.

When is your time of harvest? If yours comes weekly, as in a weekly paycheck, I think that first fruit offering, that ceremony and that singing in our heart should be done on a weekly basis. That offering should be brought in the basket and given to the priest-pastor so he can set it before the altar. We make the confession and then take it from the altar and literally set it before God in our own heart. All this is bringing you and leading you to one primary thing: an acknowledgment of God as your Source.

I shall never forget the words of Daniel when he said to the king, "the God in whose hand thy breath is." James puts it another way. "What is your life? It is as a vapor, a puff of smoke." You see, the very air that you are breathing is a gift from God and the fact that your heart is beating, is a gift from God Almighty. Yet when it comes to what we do with our money, with our first fruits, we keep the first fruits and spend them along with the rest. And God is absolutely robbed of everything. Yet God is the One in whose hand our breath is. Is it any wonder that even though we are the seed of Abraham, we are not blessed? You cannot humble yourself in your heart and humble yourself in your confession without it affecting your pocketbook.

Abraham paid tithes to Melchizedek when there was no law to do it. He just figured that it was in his best interest to do it. When you humble yourself down before God, nobody has got to get up and preach a tithing sermon. I mean, it just goes with the territory. I recognize God as *the source* of my breath, my heartbeat, my health, my car, my clothes, my home, my family, my livelihood, my church, my money; it is all from God. I am nothing and have nothing and possess nothing and claim nothing. It all comes from God and it is all going to go back to God. This is the law of the first fruits.

Finally, we come to the place where he asks, "Look down from thy holy habitation, from heaven, and bless thy people." See verse 15 above. He didn't dare ask this until he had gone through the ceremonies of the first fruits. Once he had done that and meant it from his heart, Moses felt he was in a good position to ask God to bless his people. So he said, "look down and bless."

Verse 16 declares that "This day the Lord thy God has commanded thee to do these [things]: thou shalt, therefore, keep and do them with all thine heart and with all thine soul. [And in so doing], thou hast avouched the Lord this day to be thy God and to walk in his ways, to keep his statues, his commandments, his ordinances, and to harken to his voice."

Deut 26:17
**17 Thou hast avouched the LORD this day to be thy God, and
to walk in his ways, and to keep his statutes, and his commandments, and his judgments, and to hearken unto his voice: (KJV)**

By your doing that, the Lord hath avowed thee this day to be His
peculiar people as He has promised thee and that thou shall keep all
of His commandments. For God will "make thee high above all
nations which He has made, in praise, and in name, and in honor; and
that thou mayest be an holy people unto the Lord thy God, as He has
spoken," *all contingent upon and wrapped up in the law of the
offering of the first fruits.*

Deut 26:18-19
**18 And the LORD hath avouched thee this day to be his pecu-
liar people, as he hath promised thee, and thou shouldest keep all his
commandments;**
**19 And to make thee high above all nations which he hath
made, in praise, and in name, and in honour; and that thou mayest
be an holy people unto the LORD thy God, as he hath spoken.
(KJV)**

When you don't give God the first fruits, when He has devoted a
whole chapter to it, you cut yourself off from every blessing men-
tioned above in verses 15 through 19. Obviously, you are the big
loser.

You must now, dear reader, answer the obvious question. Do you
want to be blessed? Do you want what God so plainly says in His
word belongs to you? Do you want His will done for your life? This
will include provision beyond your wildest dreams. He promises
"filled barns" and "bursting presses" based upon your stewardship of
the first fruits.

Prov 3:9-10

9 Honour the LORD with thy substance, and with the first fruits of all thine increase:

10 So shall thy barns be filled with plenty, and thy presses shall burst out with new wine. (KJV)

When you received Jesus as your personal Savior, you believed what the Bible said about Him, and you acted upon that information. Consequently, you were saved as a result of it. Why will you not also believe what the Bible says about blessings and provision for you now that you are saved? Why not act out the information contained in this book just as you acted out the information concerning Jesus as your Savior? Once you act on any part of God's Word, that part of it supernaturally translates itself into reality. Begin now to pay your tithe, give your offerings and perform everything pertaining to the first fruits offering. Then watch blessings supernaturally begin to come your way.

Don't be so naive as to cling to this little cliché, "Well, that's Old Testament." Let me tell you something. What's Old Testament to the God of the Abrahamic Covenant and to the people of the Abrahamic Covenant, unless the New Testament has plainly set it aside, applies to New Testament people who are grafted right into the Old Testament Abrahamic System. So not only is the tithe, the offering, and the first fruits offering not set aside, but you are grafted right smack into the middle of all three of them. When you throw this up at me, "Well, that's Old Testament," that is just another way of saying to me and to yourself, "I'm not going to humble myself and give God the credit that is due Him. I am going to keep the first fruits." There's your problem, not that it is Old Testament. It's not a problem of where in Scripture it is discussed. It's a problem of what's wrong in your heart. Because when those Scriptures speak in the Old Testament to the Abrahamic Seed Group, you have been grafted into it, and it is still valid for today. And unless the cross sets aside

71

something from the Old Testament, we are part and parcel of it. The cross has never set aside the tithe, the offerings, and the law of the First Fruits Offering. We are in it.

Now if you doubt that, try it, and see what happens. Act it out and see if the blessings won't come your way. I mean it is just this simple. The proof is in the pudding. It's a fact that Jesus did away with the Law. But it is also a fact that the Holy Ghost has written it in our hearts now. The blessing part is still valid and we are included in it. Do it. Act on it. Move out upon it and see what comes your way. Failure to do so is a matter of not acknowledging God as your Source and not honoring Him with your first fruits.

If I act on the above, God is obligated, based on the Abrahamic Covenant, to see me through. You see, when I discovered that Abraham paid tithes to Melchizedek before Moses ever gave the law, that said something to me because I have grappled with this thing as hard as any man. Let's face it. I don't want to tithe. I would rather keep all the money myself. You know we are like that, aren't we? I would justify my selfish attitude by saying, "I am not under the Law. I don't have to do that." Then it came to me. Abraham paid tithes when there was no law that made him do it. Why did Abraham do that? You will know why he did it once you look at what God did for Abraham, one of the most blessed men in the world. Consequently, there must be something to this.

So don't tell me this is Old Testament. No, that is not your problem. Your problem is your heart. You are eating your seed. You are spending God's money and trying to justify it. You wonder why you are always on the outside looking in, barely in the perimeter. You are sort of a fringe Christian. This gets down where it hurts, doesn't it? I can speak this way because I have been on both sides of this thing. I have learned the hard way that I would rather do it

72

God's Way. If I do it His Way, He is obligated to help me. If I do it my way, He is not obligated to help me at all. I am strictly on my own and that is a bad way to be, especially when you are a preacher; that's really bad. I can preach it. But I can't put the power to it. So I have to be obedient, because if I am not, there is no power. It's just words. So, the third step you must take to claim Abrahamic blessings is make an offering of your first fruits in addition to your tithe and your other offerings.

I have given you some instructions concerning the first fruits. Study them carefully. Look them over again. Read them over many times. Go back through them often. You will see things that I didn't even bring out, because I just hit the high points. When that first fruit offering is done right, then we have the right to say, "Father, look down from heaven and bless your people."

Chapter Five

The Fourth Step You Must Take
To Claim Abrahamic Blessings

In the book of Second Corinthians 4:3-7, Paul said, "if our gospel be hidden, it is hidden to them that are lost." Then, he says why in verse four. He said the lost are those "in whom the god of this world [or age] hath blinded the minds of them which believe not, lest the light of the glorious gospel of Christ, who is the image of God, should shine unto them."

> **2 Cor 4:3-7**
> **3 But if our gospel be hid, it is hid to them that are lost:**
> **4 In whom the god of this world hath blinded the minds of**
> **them which believe not, lest the light of the glorious gospel of Christ,**
> **who is the image of God, should shine unto them.**
> **5 For we preach not ourselves, but Christ Jesus the Lord; and**
> **ourselves your servants for Jesus' sake.**
> **6 For God, who commanded the light to shine out of dark-**
> **ness, hath shined in our hearts, to give the light of the knowledge of**
> **the glory of God in the face of Jesus Christ.**
> **7 But we have this treasure in earthen vessels, that the excel-**
> **lency of the power may be of God....**
> **(KJV)**

When you consider this passage beyond just a superficial reading, it's absolutely staggering what Paul said in these few verses. It's a fact that the gospel is hidden. But what is so sobering is the reason why it defies logic. He says if our gospel is hidden, it is hidden *because the god of this world, the devil, has blinded the minds of the lost.*

75

This is one of the most staggering statements in all the Scripture to describe the plight of a person who is not saved. The Bible said that person has had a number done on his brain by the devil. Now, the word "devil" is not used here. But who else is the god of this world, or the god of this age? John tells us that the whole world lieth in the "lap" of the wicked one. He cradles the world because he is the god of this world. He's called that in other places. The god of this age is the devil and he does a number on the brain of the lost person. The devil blinds his mind. In other words, the devil blinds the minds of the lost.

When we were born into the stream of human existence, we were born with our minds in that blind condition. This is exactly what happened to Adam and Eve in the garden when they sinned, and then passed it on to us. Consequently, our minds are blinded to the things of God from birth. For that reason, the gospel is hidden. It's hidden because our minds have had a number done on them by the devil. That number stops the light of the gospel from shining upon us. It said, "lest the light of the glorious gospel of Christ should shine" onto them. It's as though there was a light to be turned on in our minds, a light that comes only from God to dispel this darkness, to dispel this blinding business. That light must turn on in order for us to ever know, receive, and understand the things of God.

Notice closely what I'm about to say. Verse 6 says, "For God who commanded the light to shine out of darkness has shined in our hearts to give us the light of the knowledge of the gospel of Jesus Christ." In other words, *God shines in the hearts but not the minds* of those of us who are believers. He turned on a light in our *hearts but not our minds* that we might have the light of the gospel and everything that goes with it. But until God turns on that light in our *hearts (He does not turn the light on in our minds)*, the things of God are hidden away from us. Now here is the tragedy. Since man has had his mind blinded and can only understand and perceive and know and receive the things of God by a Holy Ghost light being turned on inside his heart, we can see then the necessity of having our minds renewed in some way, *because God does not turn any light on inside our minds.*

Therefore, for us to know, understand and receive the things of God, we literally, absolutely, must have two things: 1. God's light turned on inside of us. 2. A mind that has been renewed in some way, since *God's light affects our heart but not our mind.*

When you get saved, the first thing that happens is God supernaturally recreates your spirit. He makes your spirit come alive to the things of God. That's the light turning on.

The second thing that happens is the Spirit of God comes inside that recreated spirit of yours and begins to live.

The third thing that happens is, the Holy Ghost reveals to your recreated spirit the fact that the Bible is the Word of God. Consequently, these three: your spirit, the Spirit of God, and the Scripture, all have lined up in agreement at this point. They are all in harmony.

But, your mind is still the same mind even after you get saved. It is still the same mind you had before you were born again. Therefore, what had to happen next is you have to get your mind renewed so that your mind, as a new Christian, lines up in harmony and complete agreement with your spirit, the Spirit of God, and the Word of God. When your mind is renewed, all four: your mind, your spirit, the Spirit of God, and the Word of God, will be in harmony on every subject. But until this harmonization occurs, your mind is not renewed in certain areas.

There has to be a turning on of the light. Then there has to be a renewal of the mind in every area concerning the things of God. Otherwise you will not know, understand, or receive them even though you've been saved. You will wear the denominational and traditional blinders. You will listen to what they say and that's all. You must renew your own mind and bring it into line with the Word of God, the Spirit of God, and your own recreated spirit.

When your mind begins to get renewed, here's what happens: God begins to reveal to you the truth of certain scriptures, certain portions of His Word. As He does this He makes that key portion of His Word "grab you." He makes it "come alive" to you. When it "grabs you" or "comes alive" to you, you begin to think, at least in that specific area, according to the Word of God, not according to tradition or even according to your own logic.

What exactly is the renewed mind, and how do I get it? First, let me define what it is and from this definition you will also know how to get it. A renewed mind is a mind that is so saturated with Scripture that no matter what comes into your environment and circumstances, it responds with Scripture.

Sometimes things happen in my life and my natural thinking hits a panic button. But when my mind is renewed, I don't hit the panic button. I think Scripture rather than circumstance, and I deal with that circumstance according to the Word of God. In other words, a renewed mind is a mind that has been reprogrammed with Scripture to the place that it automatically thinks Scripture rather than human logic.

The natural man lives by his wits. And, unfortunately, a carnal

Christian is simply a Christian who has a renewed spirit that is in harmony with the Holy Ghost, both of which are in full agreement with the Word of God. But his mind is still out there in left field. It's not renewed. It's not been reprogrammed with Scripture. He still hits the panic button. He still lives by his wits. In other words, his mind is not in harmony with these other three. That guy is as saved as anybody, but he is carnal. He lives by his wits.

A renewed mind is the mind of a saved man that has been reprogrammed with the Word of God. It is a mind that has had every cell laced with the Word of God to the place where it doesn't think on its own anymore. It thinks Scripture. That person has a mind that is now in harmony with the Word of God, the Spirit of God, and his own recreated spirit. When these four are in harmony, that Christian is a conqueror. Nothing can stop him/her!

But, when his mind is still a renegade doing its own thing, thinking its own thoughts, living by its own wits, that mind is dominating his spirit. It's pulling his spirit away, and the spirit of that saved man is lining up with his unrenewed mind. For his mind is dominating his spiritual life. He's living by his wits. When he lives by his wits, he is living religiously. He may be very religious, but he has on religious blinders that are composed of his religious background or his religious tradition. He has not renewed his mind yet to the things of God.

We are born with this unrenewed mind. That's how we come into this world. The devil has blinded the minds of them which believe not. And unfortunately, when you get saved, this blindness is not immediately dispelled. It requires the renewing process which consists of learning and knowing the Scripture to the place where thinking Scripture becomes as automatic to you as breathing. At this "automatic" point, then, this person has a renewed mind. But the Christian who has not reached the "automatic" point is a person who means well. He may be very religious but his mind is out in left field and does not line up with anything except doing its own thing. There's not a dime's worth of difference between the way that person thinks and the way a lost man thinks. They both live by their wits. Both minds are blinded.

Now, since a new Christian's mind is still blinded, and it is not completely renewed at the new birth, he is in a mess. He's got to get straightened out which can only be done by bringing his mind into harmony with the Word of God, the Spirit of God, and his own recreated spirit. The Bible calls all this **THE RENEWING OF THE MIND.**

Let's go now to the book of First Corinthians, Chapter 2. Paul says the same thing in this letter. He said in Verse 9, "Eye hath not seen, nor ear heard, neither have entered into the heart of man, [that is a natural man], the things which God hath prepared for them that love him."

> **1 Cor 2:9-16**
> **9 But as it is written, Eye hath not seen, nor ear heard, neither have entered into the heart of man, the things which God hath prepared for them that love him.**
> **10 But God hath revealed them unto us by his Spirit: for the Spirit searcheth all things, yea, the deep things of God.**
> **11 For what man knoweth the things of a man, save the spirit of man which is in him? even so the things of God knoweth no man, but the Spirit of God.**
> **12 Now we have received, not the spirit of the world, but the spirit which is of God; that we might know the things that are freely given to us of God.**
> **13 Which things also we speak, not in the words which man's wisdom teacheth, but which the Holy Ghost teacheth; comparing spiritual things with spiritual.**

14 But the natural man receiveth not the things of the Spirit of God: for they are foolishness unto him: neither can he know them, because they are spiritually discerned.
15 But he that is spiritual judgeth all things, yet he himself is judged of no man.
16 For who hath known the mind of the Lord, that he may instruct him? But we have the mind of Christ. **(KJV)**

There is a mountain of spiritual truth we don't know about because we've been trying to know it with our natural minds, with our wits, with our unrenewed mind. That is a person whose religion causes this reaction; if he gets around a spiritual person he will almost be willing to kill and think he's done God a service because that person's spiritual life contradicts and antagonizes his own carnal life. Consequently, he does not like it and he cannot help himself for his mind is still blinded. It's not renewed yet by the Word of God.

He's religious but he is as carnal as a goat. For everything that he knows comes through his brain. And you can't know the things of God from your brain. You don't get the things of God into your brain from seeing it, from tasting it, from smelling it, from feeling it, or from hearing it. For the five senses go into your brain and that's not where the things of God are known. They are known through the spirit of man as the mind of that man lines up with it. The spirit of man, the Holy Ghost, and the Word of God cannot penetrate and control your whole being until your mind is brought into harmony with them by the renewal process.

Verse 10, above, says that God reveals the things of God to the spiritual Christian by His Spirit. That's the only way we get it. For "the Spirit searcheth all things yea, [even] the deep things of God." It's the Spirit of God revealing things to our human spirit that has been recreated. And He reveals the Word of God to us. He makes the

81

Scriptures come alive in our spirit. Your part in this renewal of the mind process is to lace your own brain with Scripture so that what your spirit knows, your mind can bear witness with. Your mind can be brought into harmony only by saturating it with the Scripture.

Now look at verse 12 which says, "we have received not the spirit of the world but the spirit who is of God that we might know the things of God."

I want to ask you a question. If the mind of man is blinded to the place where he cannot know the things of God, and if that blinding process was done by the devil, and if it is impossible for us to know the things of God until the Spirit of God does something to us which enables us to know them, then my question to you is this: How much of our thought life is original? How much of what you think is really you thinking it? Let me ask it another way. How much of your thought life was placed in your brain by the devil? Or, how much of what you think was placed there by the Spirit of God? Or again, the original question, how much of what I think is original if my mind is blinded to the place where the things of God are hidden from me, totally out of view, and if the only way I can know them is by the Spirit of God revealing them to me? This says to me that my natural brain can never know them. So when it comes to the spirit realm or any realm, how much of what you think, ladies and gentlemen, was placed in your brain by you? You think you're thinking it, but how much of what you think are you really responsible for? This is sobering. To consider that what I think may be simply a preconceived computer program of the devil, who slipped his own disk into my brain, is sobering. So how much of what you think is really you? If God's Spirit has to tamper with me to enable me to think the things of God, because the devil has already tampered with me so that the things of God are totally hidden from me, how much of what I do and think and say is original with me?

82

Here is where I'm going with this. Religion and tradition say that it is not God's will for a Christian to be wealthy. This book has laid this nonsense to rest. Tradition and religion also say that God won't necessarily heal a sick Christian. Consequently, when the average Christian gets sick he'll pray, "If it be Thy will, Lord, heal me." Well, anybody that knows the Scripture can just lace your brain down like a football with healing scriptures demonstrating emphatically that it is the will of God for you to be healed. But you see, the devil has programmed your mind with tradition that says, "Well now, it just might not be God's will to heal you. You better pray, 'if it be thy will.'"

Have you ever stopped to analyze what you are doing when you pray to God, "if it be thy will"? What He spelled out in the Scripture is most definitely His will, and you can pray for it without saying that faith destroying phrase, "if it be Thy will."

What you are saying to God with this ridiculous phrase is this: "I don't believe what Your Word says. I know that Peter said, and Isaiah said, one in past tense, one in present tense, that by His stripes we were and are healed. I know that, but I don't believe either of them."

What you are saying when you insert that, "if it be Thy will," is this: "God, I don't believe a word of what the Bible says, but, Lord, in case I'm wrong in my unbelief, in case I'm wrong about calling Your book a lie, in case I'm wrong about this and it really is Your will, then go ahead and heal me, because I sure would like to be." That's what you are doing.

But, you say that you didn't stop to analyze this. Well, why haven't you? Because your mind is as blind as a bat, and this blindness was caused by the devil. The Bible says our minds have been blinded by the god of this age and that we're born into that condition. So we figure things out with our wits. But in so doing we will be deceived and we'll go against what the Scriptures teach. So what we are saying with this "if it be thy will" nonsense is this: "God, if I'm mistaken, if I'm mistaken in my unbelief, if You really meant that, then go ahead and heal me, because I sure would like to be. So if it is Thy will and I'm really wrong about it, and You really mean it, and it really is Your will, then I want You to heal me."

You see that's not a prayer of faith. That's unbelief. Find out what the Word of God says and lace your mind with it. For only then is your mind renewed in that specific area. Then act on what it says, and God Almighty will heal you or prosper you or anything else covered in His Word. I can get a person healed and prospered if I can change their thinking. And I can change their thinking if I can get their mind renewed in that area by teaching them what the Bible says concerning those areas.

Let me shift gears. Before you can get saved, you have to have a renewal process going in your mind about Jesus Christ. You have to "see" for yourself that Jesus wasn't after you to zap you. He died for your sins that you might be saved. When you came into an awareness of this, a light "turned on" inside you. God turned that light on. And then you received Jesus Christ as your personal Savior. But before that could happen, you had to have some information about it. Jesus died for you wherever you are right now. You can be saved. He is the Son of God. And he did die for your sins.

I'm reprogramming your mind right at this point. He does not want to hurt you. Jesus came to save you. Jesus is not mad at you. He loves you. Jesus does not hate you; he cares about you. God loves you. He does not want to damn you. He does not want to see you in hell. Now there is some information. That's the word of God that will reprogram your thinking if you'll let it. And if you will just let it, God will use what I just said and turn on a light in your heart, and the light of the glorious Gospel of Jesus Christ will suddenly shine and you can receive Him as your Savior right where you are.

"Well, Jay, how do I receive Him as my Savior?" Simply bow your head, and pray this prayer with me:

Dear Jesus Christ, forgive me of my sins. I believe you are the Savior of the world, and I'm asking you to save my soul from hell and forgive my sins. Jesus, forgive me. And save me.

And wherever you are right now, He'll do it. He will save you.

Next, we need to consider some things about the mind renewal from the book of Mark, chapter 11:22-23. This is a classic passage. I want to point out some things that maybe you haven't seen before. My job is to build your faith, and I do everything I can to do that. So let's begin at verse 22.

> **Mark 11:22-23**
> **22 And Jesus answering saith unto them, Have faith in God.**
> **23 For verily I say unto you, That whosoever shall say unto this mountain, Be thou removed, and be thou cast into the sea; and shall not doubt in his heart, but shall believe that those things which he saith shall come to pass; he shall have whatsoever he saith.**
> **(KJV)**

Let me give you some background. The day before this passage, Jesus saw a fig tree which had no figs on it and He cursed it. He said in verse 14, "No man eateth from thee, hereafter forever." And His disciples heard it. Well, the next day they were coming back down the same road and saw this fig tree. It was dried up from the

85

roots. They were astonished. Peter, remembering, said unto Him, "Master behold the fig tree which thou curseth is withered away." Then Jesus said, "Have faith in God." And then He said, "Verily, verily, I say unto you, That whosoever shall say unto this mountain, Be thou removed and be thou cast into the sea and shall not doubt in his heart but shall believe that those things which he sayeth shall come to pass; he shall have whatever he saith."

Now, this is a staggering statement; it is one of the most staggering statements in Scripture. But it must be understood in the light of the simple expression in verse 22, "Have faith in God." But what does this mean in this context? In order to answer this question, we must have a working definition of "faith."

So I'm going to give you the Bible definition of faith. You need to write this down in your Bible. What is faith? *Faith is knowing the will of God in advance. Believing is acting on that revelation. "Faith" is a noun. It's information. "Believe" is a verb. It's something you do based on that information. Faith is information received from God for you to act upon.* You are a believer or you believe that information when you act upon it. Jesus had some information from God about that fig tree. Although we are not told specifically in the text, we know it by the real meaning of the word, "faith." Have faith in God. In other words, what He is saying is this: "You saw me curse a fig tree, you saw me say something to that fig tree but what you don't realize is that what I said is based on what God told me. And God said to me, I don't want that fig tree around; it's cluttering up the ground. It doesn't produce figs. Curse it so that it dies and nothing ever grows on it again, forever." In other words, Jesus is simply saying that His cursing of the fig tree was the information that He had received from God for Him to act upon. And He said, "I simply did what God said to me in my spirit." So He said to them, "You must have the same kind of faith, or information from God.

86

You *must* have this information from God."

But here is an area where the translation is not as plain as it needs to be. It says, "Have faith *in* God." But what it says from the Greek text is, "Have faith *from* God." "In" is a Greek ablative. The ablative in Greek designates the *source* of something. The information, which makes up what the Bible calls "faith" must come from God as the source of it. So what Jesus is saying is this: "You marvel that I was able to say something to a fig tree and what I said happened to it." He said, "You may have a mountain come along in your life like that fig tree came along in mine. You need to have a message from God about your mountain like I had about this fig tree."

You *must* have a word from God. That's what you must have. You must have a word from God, for when you get that word or information from God, you can say to your mountain the content of that information (what God said to you), and whatever God has said to you is going to be the outcome of that mountain. Say that information to your mountain, and it will happen. It will happen, not just because you say it, but because God said it and you agree with it. That's the background here.

Now, in order for me to say something to my mountain based on the Word of God and based on knowledge or information I received from God, I have to, first of all, have that information. I have been talking about the renewed mind and I am still on that subject, because everybody's mind hasn't been renewed yet. Listen to me. A renewed mind is the mind of a Christian that's been brought into harmony with three things. For you see when you first get saved, God recreates your spirit. He brings it alive to the things of God.

Second, He sends His Holy Ghost inside of your spirit that had been recreated and His Holy Ghost lives inside of your spirit.

Third, the Holy Ghost reveals the Scripture to your spirit. So, those three are in harmony. Now your mind, unfortunately, was not completely brought into harmony with all these three the moment you got saved. So your mind has to be renewed. Once again, let me give you the definition of the renewed mind. A Christian's mind has been renewed when that mind is laced with the Word of God, when it is so saturated with the Word of God that when something comes into your environment, (a mountain or a fig tree), your mind responds with Scripture. In other words, a renewed mind is a Christian's mind that has become so saturated with Scripture that when something presents itself, he automatically responds and thinks and plots a course of action based on Scripture, not on his wits.

Now this is done two ways. You mind is saturated with Scripture as you listen to sermons, messages, as you study the Bible, as you fellowship with Christian people, as you talk about the Scripture, as you attend church, and as you listen in Sunday School classes. As you expose your mind to the Word of God, your mind becomes saturated. It will never be saturated with Scripture beyond the level of your exposure to Scripture. And as much as I am for studying Scripture on your own, I believe listening to preaching is as important a thing as you can do, because there is something about the spoken Word that penetrates the cells of the human mind and spirit. So you need to hear sermons, Spirit-filled sermons by Spirit-filled preachers that put content in their messages, preachers that have something to say. Your mind must have something more than jumping up and down and hollering and feeling good. That's how you begin the process. Now the second phase of this process is this: You have to get to the place where you recognize your own ability to speak out loud and tell your brain what to think. You have to literally get to the place where you force your mind with the spoken Word what to think. You see, your mind is a renegade. Your mind will run off out there on its own and you will begin to operate by your wits. And when you, a Christian, operate by your wits, you are a carnal Christian. I don't care how religious you are, how many denominations you belong to, and how big a deacon you are in your church. When you operate with your brain, you are a carnal Christian.

A Christian who operates with his wits is a person who has not had his mind renewed. There's not a dime's worth of difference in the way he thinks and bases his life and the way a lost man thinks and bases his life, for both of them operate strictly by their wits. I am saying to you that you must have your mind renewed by saturating it with Scripture and then forcing it to line up with your spirit, the Holy Ghost, and the Word of God, and *by telling it what it must think* in the light of Scripture.

We see the importance of *speaking* the Will of God. Jesus did it and said you can do it to a mountain. But, there are three things of extreme importance for us to know. First, you have to know the Mind of God on a specific subject. Second, you have to speak the Mind of God on a specific subject. And third, you cannot doubt in your heart about the Mind of God on a specific subject.

Now, let's concentrate on the expression in verse 23, "shall not doubt in his heart." There are two words we must fully understand in this expression. First, the word translated "doubt" is one Greek word which combines two Greek words. It is the Greek word for "through," combined with the Greek word to "separate" or to "divide." It means, then, to separate thoroughly or to divide through and through. The second word is "heart" which is used here as an exact synonym for "spirit" or your recreated spirit.

What Jesus means, then, in this expression, "and shall not doubt in his heart" is this:

1. Your heart or spirit is the place in your being where God reveals His Will to you.

2. The Word of God, the Spirit of God and your recreated spirit or heart are lined up and in harmony.

3. When your mind has not been renewed, there is a thorough division (doubt) between what your unrenewed mind thinks and what your recreated spirit knows to be the Word and Will of God.

4. Your unrenewed mind attempts to pull your recreated spirit away from agreement with the Word and Spirit of God and entice it, even overwhelm it, into agreement with itself.

5. At the point your unrenewed mind accomplishes this, your mind has dominated your recreated spirit. As such, the following becomes the case.

6. There is now a total division (doubt) in this manner: your unrenewed mind and recreated spirit are lined up as partners in agreement. They stand against the Word and Spirit of God.

7. The result is this: your unrenewed mind has dominated your spirit so that inside your being there is a total division of two against two. Your renegade mind and spirit are divided against the Word and Spirit of God.

8. The tragedy here is this: when this two-by-two division occurs, your mouth will speak into existence the things your unrenewed mind thinks, which is just more of what is already in your circumstances and environment.

You cannot thoroughly separate your heart from what you think in your mind. In other words, there can be no cleavage in your spirit man between what you think and what God said. You have to think what God said. For when you are separated in your spirit from what God said, that's the place where your spirit is dominated by your renegade, unrenewed mind.

Then the four things (the Word and Spirit of God, your spirit and mind) are not lined up. There is a division, two-by-two. Your spirit becomes separated and lines up with your unrenewed mind because the mind has overpowered your recreated spirit and dictates to it. The Word of God and the Holy Ghost are saying one thing, and your unrenewed mind, which has drawn your spirit away from those two, is saying something else. So, your inner being which should be all lined up and in harmony is divided thoroughly down the middle. You have two and two. You have your unrenewed mind dictating to your recreated spirit, which separates from the Word of God and the Holy Ghost. The Spirit of God and the Word of God are saying one thing and your unrenewed mind, having forced your spirit to line up with it, is on a different wave length entirely. There is division.

What Jesus is saying is this: Do not be divided thoroughly in the area of your spirit man, which is what the word "heart" means in the New Testament. For you see, your mind must line up with the other three. But the carnal Christian is a person whose unrenewed mind pulls his spirit away from the Spirit of God and the Word of God so that the spirit is dominated by his renegade, unrenewed mind. When this occurs, you are going to speak the opposite of what the Word of God says. For Jesus says, you have to "say to" your fig tree or mountain based on the revealed Will of God.

So, when I am speaking the Word of God, it shows that my mind has been renewed and is so laced with Scripture that my mind is lined up with my spirit, the Spirit of God, and the Word of God to the point where my mouth is dominated and controlled by these four. *When all four are in harmony, my mouth will "say" the things of God.* When I am believing God's word or information to the point where I "say" it, *it happens.*

91

But, when my unrenewed mind pulls my spirit away from the Word of God and the Holy Ghost, then my speech is a reflection of these two, divided and separated completely from the other two. And what I say is exactly what I get.

I read one author who said that Jesus made the statement that you can have what you say, but most people go around saying what they *already have.* When they "say" what they *already have,* this reflects the fact that there has already been this division thoroughly in the heart. For the unrenewed mind has pulled the heart, the recreated spirit of that Christian, away from its mooring, its anchor, which is the Word of God and the Spirit of God. And whichever way this combination works, that's what you are going to "say." And when your unrenewed mind has pulled your spirit away from the Word and Spirit of God, you are going to "say" the opposite of what the Scriptures "say," for you are going to operate on tradition, denominationalism, religious blinders, and commonsense. You are operating logically, and not spiritually, and that person is not a spiritual man. There has been a cleavage or a division in the realm of the spirit man or the heart, and his heart has been pulled away. When the mind has been renewed, and it is lined up with your spirit, the Word of God, and the Holy Ghost, you can and will "say" what God "says" and get it. Then it will become true for you. You can have what you "say" based on the Word of God.

When your mind dominates your spirit, it divides it away from the Spirit of God and the Word of God. Then, *it controls your mouth,* and you will "say" negative things. You will "say" the *opposite of what the Word of God says and then that is what you will have.*

In other words, you get sick. Maybe it is a terminal disease. The Word of God says that it is the Will of God for His children to be healed. Period. There are no exceptions to that statement, regardless of what so and so happens to say about it. That is a fact. When your mind becomes renewed in the area of what God's Word says about healing, your mind is going to line up with your spirit which already knows this truth and the Holy Ghost which knows this truth and the Word of God which teaches this truth. Your mind is going to line up with these three and you are going to find one healing scripture (one is all it takes), and you are going to "say" or confess that one scripture because, now, there is a four-part harmony: your renewed mind, the Word of God, the Holy Ghost, and your spirit. And guess what? You are going to have what you "say," which is healing. You are going to have it because it is the Word of God, it's your faith, it's your information, and when you "say" it, you act on it.

But, you folks that are wearing religious blinders, those blinders are composed of human logic, not the Word of God, not the scripture. Your unrenewed mind that is as carnal as a goat, that operates purely in its own natural realm just like a lost person, is going to woo your spirit away from its mooring, which is the Word of God and the Holy Ghost, and force it under the dominion of that unrenewed, renegade, logical mind.

When that occurs you are going to start praying, "If it be Thy will, oh God, please heal me." Do you know what you do when you pray, "if it be Thy will?" What you are saying is simple, it is very simple. You are saying in your unrenewed mind, "I don't believe a word of Scripture that says "by His stripes I am healed," but Lord, in case I am mistaken when I go right in the face of what Your Word says, when I call your Word a lie if I am making a mistake, then if it is Thy Will, dear God, please heal me because I sure want to be."

That's what you are saying. I have people get angry at me over that. I could care less, man, I am trying to help you. I know traditional, religious blinders. I wore them long enough. Thank God, I was delivered from them. Your mind has to be renewed or it will pull your spirit away. Then you will "say" the opposite of what God's Word says. You will curse no fig tree, you will move no mountain, you won't be healed, you will not prosper and claim Abrahamic blessings, you will amount to nothing.

There may be some of you who have never been saved. You have never received Jesus as your personal Savior. Your mind has been blinded to this particular truth of God. You believe Jesus wants to hurt you, wants to zap you, that He is mad at you over your sins, that He is just full of wrath, and that He is floating around the skies all day hunting somebody to zap over the fact that they did something wrong. That was my idea for years. Let me tell you something. God loves you. Jesus died for your sins because He loves you. And He wants to save you.

Do you know that I have baptized more than one convicted murderer that I have led to Christ? They had murdered people. I won them to Christ and baptized them. They finished their sentences and now they are out of prison and are upstanding citizens. You see, God wants to forgive you through the blood of Jesus. So wherever you are right now, why don't you just bow your head, ask Jesus to forgive your sins and be your Savior. Why don't you just say, "Dear Jesus, I do believe that You are the Son of God and I do believe You died for my sins, and I do believe that God raised You from the dead." Then, ask Him to save your soul from hell. He will.

Back to our subject of claiming Abrahamic blessings, your fourth step is to renew your mind with prosperity Scriptures in addition to giving your tithes, offerings and your first fruits offerings.

Chapter Six

The Fifth Step You Must Take
To Claim Abrahamic Blessings

Mark 4:3-9 contains the parable of the sower sowing the seed and the various kinds of ground in which the seed fell. In this chapter, we shall see some things that you probably have not seen before. That "something" is the last thing you must do to claim Abrahamic blessings.

> **Mark 4:3-9**
> **3 Hearken; Behold, there went out a sower to sow:**
> **4 And it came to pass, as he sowed, some fell by the way side, and the fowls of the air came and devoured it up.**
> **5 And some fell on stony ground, where it had not much earth; and immediately it sprang up, because it had no depth of earth:**
> **6 But when the sun was up, it was scorched; and because it had no root, it withered away.**
> **7 And some fell among thorns, and the thorns grew up, and choked it, and it yielded no fruit.**
> **8 And other fell on good ground, and did yield fruit that sprang up and increased; and brought forth, some thirty, and some sixty, and some an hundred.**
> **9 And he said unto them, He that hath ears to hear, let him hear. (KJV)**

It's verse 8 that we really want to concentrate on. "And other fell on good ground. And did yield fruit that sprang up and increased and brought forth some thirty and some sixty and some one hundred." This seed fell on good ground. It sprang up, increased, and brought forth fruit. Some of that seed brought forth 30-fold fruit, some of it brought forth 60, and some of it brought forth 100. And then Jesus makes a strange statement in verse 9, linking verse 9 to verse 8, when He says, "He that hath ears to hear, let him hear." When the disciples were alone with Him, they asked Him about the parable. He said unto them:

Mark 4:11

11 And he said unto them, Unto you it is given to know the mystery of the kingdom of God: but unto them that are without, all these things are done in parables: (KJV)

Now Jesus says something else here. There is a group to whom it is given to know the things of God. There is also a group that this is not given to. So Jesus said, "He that hath ears to hear, let him hear," and the rest of them can't. Now having said that let's get Jesus' interpretation of this parable.

Mark 4:14-20

14 The sower soweth the word.

15 And these are they by the way side, where the word is sown; but when they have heard, Satan cometh immediately, and taketh away the word that was sown in their hearts.

16 And these are they likewise which are sown on stony ground; who when they have heard the word, immediately receive it with gladness;

17 And have no root in themselves, and so endure but for a time: afterward, when affliction or persecution ariseth for the word's sake, immediately they are offended.

18 And these are they which are sown among thorns; such as hear the word,

19 And the cares of this world, and the deceitfulness of riches, and the lusts of other things entering in, choke the word, and it becometh unfruitful.

20 And these are they which are sown on good ground; such as hear the word, and receive it, and bring forth fruit, some thirtyfold, some

sixty, and some an hundred.

21 And he said unto them, is a candle brought to be put under a bushel, or under a bed? and not to be set on a candlestick?

22 For there is nothing hid, which shall not be manifested; neither was any thing kept secret, but that it should come aboard.

23 If any man have ears to hear, let him hear.

24 And he said unto them, Take heed what ye hear: with what measure ye mete, it shall be measured to you: and unto you that hear shall more be given. (KJV)

Jesus said in verse 14, "The sower soweth the Word." Now the Word that's being sown here is the Word of God. It's God's Word. It's Scripture. It's the Word. The sower soweth the Word.

Now let's see Jesus' interpretation, or definition, in verse 20 of "the good ground." "These are they which are sown on good ground," and He then defines, or interprets, the meaning of "the good ground." The good ground is that ground which hears the Word and receives it. The good ground is, of course, people. But it's the person that not only hears the Word but receives it. In all the other kinds of ground, and there are three of them, these two things are missing. In order for a person to be categorized as good ground for the Word of God to produce the 30, 60, and 100-fold, you have to not only hear the Word, but you have to receive it. For if you receive it, you will begin to act on it. And it's the hearing, and the receiving, and the acting on what you hear and receive that causes the seed to multiply itself. There must to be a sowing. I am doing that for you right now with this book. Second, there must also be some ground. That's you. Third, there must be some seed. The seed is the Word of God which is what I am writing. It takes all three things. You can be ground. I can be a sower, which I am. I can be putting the seed out there. You can hear it, but how you hear determines what happens in your life with it. You must not only hear it, you must receive it.

Notice verse 21. In your Bible there is a little funny looking thing at the beginning of that verse which makes it look like there is a break in content, thought pattern, and flow of thought between verse 20 and 21. But there is no break between these two verses in thought, meaning or flow. These two verses are linked together. When you see this, this whole parable will come together and make sense to you as never before. Verse 21 is a continuation of verse 20, for it says you must hear the Word and you must receive the Word. In verse 21, He asks a question: "Is a candle to be put under a bushel or under a bed and not to be set on a candle stick?" Then He said, "There is nothing hid which shall not be manifested. Neither was anything kept secret, but that it should come abroad." Then He repeats the statement He made in verse 9 which said, "If any man has ears to hear, let him hear."

In preaching soul-winning sermons, we isolate "there is nothing hidden which shall not be revealed" from the rest of this chapter and preach those evangelistic, rip-roaring, judgment messages. We usually make them say something like this: "Brother, you can't hide from God. There is nothing hidden but what is going to be revealed. God Almighty knows everything you are doing." Well, that's true but it's dead wrong in this context. Why? Let me show you something. Jesus just finished talking about the seed being the Word of God and being sown in the proper ground which hears it and receives it. Then He talks about how a candle was not made to be put under a bushel basket where you can't see it. It was not made to be put under a bed where you can't see it. But a candle is to be put right out there in broad open daylight on a candlestick where everybody can see it. Then He says in like manner there is nothing hidden that's not going to be revealed.

The book of Proverbs says that the spirit of a man is God's candle. Your spirit is God's candle.

98

Prov 20:27
27 The spirit of man is the candle of the LORD, searching all the inward parts of the belly. (KJV)

In other words, when God wants to light a light for a man, He does it in the spirit of that man. When God reveals things, He does it through your spirit, for your spirit is His candle. His candle was not made to be hidden away. His candle was made to be burning brightly for you to see. His candle is going to be burning in your spirit. To put this differently, in the Word of God there is nothing that is hidden from your spirit as a Christian. God has no secrets from us. He wants to show us everything. There is nothing that you need by way of information or instruction that God is going to be mysterious about. He's going to show it to you in your spirit. He will show it to you primarily through the sowing of the Word in the good ground that both hears and receives.

What we must understand is this: there is nothing that can be considered as "mysterious" between us and God. God will reveal Himself to you anytime, with any amount of information that you need to make your life better or to do His will.

Put all these verses together and you have the entire, deeper meaning. The good ground are those that hear the Word and receive it. And in case you are worried about receiving it, He is saying your spirit is my candle, and my candle was not meant to be hidden away but it was meant to be brightly shining. He said that is the condition of your spirit before Me, and because of that, there is nothing hidden which I will not manifest to your spirit. Neither has anything been kept secret, but that it should come abroad into your spirit. If any man will hear, let him hear what I just said. In other words, there is nothing hidden from us in the Word of God if we just hear the Word and receive it. God wants to reveal Himself to you through it. But that's not all in this context.

Notice what He says in verse 24. He said unto them, "Take heed what ye hear." Twice He has already said, "If any man has ears to hear, let him hear." Now, He is saying to that same man that has ears to hear, "Take heed what you hear." In other words, you ought to be careful what you hear. I don't like to be around negative things. Negative things generate sickness. They generate poverty. They open the door to the devil to come in and tear up everything you have going for you. I don't like negative folk, negative conversation or negative atmospheres. I don't like them. We need to take heed what we hear.

There is another side to this passage that Jesus is talking about for He doesn't stop here. He continues by talking about their "measure of hearing." He said, "with what measure you mete, it shall be measured to you." This is another Scripture that we lift out of its context and preach our evangelistic, judgement sermons on.

Notice carefully what this Scripture says. Normally we would say, "Well, with what measure you mete (or measure out) that's going to be measured back to you. In other words, brother, you get out there and you live like the devil, the devil is going to walk right back all over you and you are going to have trouble." That's very true, but not in this context. What does He mean, "With what measure you mete, it shall be measured back to you"? *He is talking about the measure of your hearing of the Word of God.* He makes this very plain in the next verse. For He says, "unto you that hear, shall more be given." So the measure that you mete that is going to be measured back to you is *determined by the limit you place upon what you hear of the Word of God.*

You see, a lot of times we hear, but we don't hear. We hear, but we tune it out. We hear, but we put limits on it. We hear, but we say, "I will go to this point and no further." We hear, but then we refuse to receive part of what we hear. We hear as far as we want to go, and then we refuse to receive further. If a fellow has his mind made up about something and all of a sudden he hears a message that goes beyond what he himself has had the time to work through and learn and appropriate, he will hear to that point and receive to that point. But he refuses to receive or hear beyond this point. *That man will have measured back to him the limit that he himself places upon his own hearing.*

Why is it some folk are healed and some are not? I believe with all my heart I have the answer to this question. I believe that when the gifts of healing are operating, whoever is silently touched by God will be healed through that gift. But what about when the gifts of healing are not operating? Then we exercise healing by faith. But it is here that some folk are not healed. They will go back to their denominational thinking and say, "I just don't believe it is the will of God for me to be healed." But, in so doing, they "heard with measures and limits." You put a measure on what the Word of God says about you personally. Consequently, the measure you place on your own hearing and receiving of what God said in His Word is the exact extent and the precise limit of which you are going to be healed by the Word of God. Why did some of this Word bring forth 30? Why did some of it bring forth 60? And why did some of it bring forth 100? Because some of those people put limits on it and others did not. They heard with a measured ear. They received with a measured receiving cup. They placed limits, and we are bound by the limits we place upon our hearing.

In this context, Jesus teaches us three things:
     1. He said twice, "he that hath ears to hear, let him hear."
     2. Then He cautions us about what we hear.

3. He counsels us about putting limits on what we hear.

You "must" hear "what" the Word says, but then you can't put a limit on the Word; you must let the Word talk about itself. Consequently, you "hear" everything that is in the Word in order to receive. Now having said that, the Word covers every area of our lives. There is no need, there is no problem that can ever present itself to you that's not covered thoroughly, completely in the Word. Now there may be a person who understands, without limits, what the Word says about salvation and he received his salvation. He is saved.

So the Bible talks about salvation. The Bible talks about healing. The Bible talks about family matters. The Bible talks about prosperity. Whatever the need is in your life is the area of the Word that you should begin to seek out to get sown into your spirit. Keep in mind I said there must be a sower, there must be some seed, which is the Word, and there must be some ground, which is your spirit. It takes all of it to make the seed grab hold and spring up, increase, and yield fruit. If there's no ground, if there's no seed, if there is no sower, it won't work. It must all be brought into action. The Word of God is useless as long as it stays in the pages of a Bible. It must get out of the pages of the Bible and be sown into the human spirit. That spirit is the candlestick of God Almighty and as you hear and receive the communication, nothing is hidden from you. So whatever your area of need is, that's the area where you need to sow.

Having laid the above foundation, I want to discuss, now, just one area: your right and ability to claim Abrahamic blessings. I absolutely believe it is the most foolish thing in the world for a Christian, a child of God, to always be down and out financially. If we are, I believe with all my heart, the reason is because we have not been hearing right. I believe if we heard right, we would not put limits

102

on it. We haven't received right, for we put up an arbitrary "measure" on our hearing concerning what the Word of God has to say about prosperity and wealth.

Because we have measured our hearing, what we "get back" in the form of fruit also has limits which are based upon the arbitrary measures we placed there when we heard. Some of us ought to be receiving a hundred and we are receiving thirty. The reason we are receiving thirty is because we put limits, we put measures for what we heard and received. We hear it, but only up to a point.

For instance, right now as you are reading this message, everybody reading is "hearing" every word with his mind. But when the Holy Ghost attempts to translate my words from the "hearing" of your "mind" into your spirit, a lot of folk are sitting out there putting brakes on it. You are measuring what you are receiving of it. Well, when you measure what you receive of the Word of God when it's being sown, you are also putting measures or limits on the amount of fruits that you "produce" as a result of the fact *you limit the sowing in your field.*

A lot of us are having it real difficult financially. Here's why. Either we don't hear or if we hear we don't receive what we heard. Or, if we receive what we hear, we put limits on it. And when you limit it, then you are placing measures on what the seed can reproduce by way of your harvest. For if you measure the amount of sowing that goes down, you are also going to measure the amount of harvest you reap. If I have five acres of land and seed enough for all five acres, and I put limits on my sowing by only sowing one acre of seed, I am only going to get back a harvest based on the sowing of one acre. But if I take the measures off and sow the whole five acres, I am going to get back five times more than I would have if I had limited myself to just one acre.

The Word of God addresses itself to every area of our lives where there might be a need. Consequently, God has to have a plan of economy in which He wants his children to prosper. Does He have such a plan? Absolutely!

I used to go around under a denominational cloud that thought God wanted everybody to be as poor as a church mouse, that nobody could be a "good" Christian unless he was "flat busted." Nobody could be right with God, I thought, unless his car wouldn't run and he didn't have a dime in his pocket. I found out, though, that I can't be a "good" Christian at all if my car won't run and I don't have a dime in my pocket. For instance, I went downtown yesterday to a store, planning to be in there less than five minutes. I got my stuff, went back to my car and started to open my car door. Then I discovered I didn't have my key. I looked through the window and there it was, still in the ignition.

This made me fire-eating mad. I am so glad that nobody called on me to pray right then. Do you see what I am talking about? Sometimes, gentle reader, we "interpret" things just plain wrong. I cannot be a "good" Christian when my car won't run for any reason. Also, I am not convinced we have to be "flat busted" to be a "good" Christian. I can be a much better Christian if I have a decent car that runs good, wear decent looking clothes, live in a decent looking house, and have enough money in my pocket to take my wife to a restaurant after church if I want to. I can be right with God a whole lot quicker and easier with things like that. You see, you can't produce one Scripture which shows that I have to be poor as Job's turkey for me to be right with God, or for me to be spiritual.

I am going to tell you something. There are multitudes of people who are right with God who are not poor as Job's turkey. But they have learned to tap the secret of an unmeasured hearing. They have found what the Word of God says about provision and blessing from God and they have taken off all the brakes, measures, and limits others put on it. They have torn down the fences. They have taken off the measures. They have unmeasured hearing and receiving. When the Word of God, which talks about their right and ability to claim blessings, is sown in their lives, these people have the seed coming up and producing in them one hundred-fold. I want the one-hundred fold.

So the Fifth Step you must take to claim Abrahamic blessings is simple. You must take heed to what you hear. You must hear it straight. You must not put limits on what you hear. You must not measure what you hear. For when you measure it, it will be measured back to you when it's time for your harvest.

Father, in the Name of Jesus bless us now financially. Amen.

Chapter Seven

God's Will Is To Make You
Extremely Blessed

Now, let me show you some things about claiming Abrahamic blessings in Second Corinthians 9:8-15, which proves the above statement once and for all.

> **2 Cor 9:8-15**
> **8 And God is able to make all grace abound toward you; that ye, always having all sufficiency in all things, may abound to every good work: (KJV)**

This question always arises, "How do I know that it is God's will for me to have blessings and provision?" The person who asks this question doesn't have a problem with God's ability to bless us abundantly. They know He has power enough to do this, "if it be Thy will." Abraham had the opposite problem. He doubted if God was able. He did not doubt that God was willing. He doubted His ability. Today, we don't doubt his ability. We doubt His *willingness*. *In the balance of this chapter, I am going to prove to you that it is the will of God for you to be blessed beyond your wildest dreams.*

Verse 8 declares that "God is able to make all grace abound toward you; that ye, always having all sufficiency in all things, may abound to every good work." Look first at the word "abound." It means to have more than enough. But this definition of "abound" does not do the word justice here. Baur, Arndt and Gingrich, on page 651 in their lexicon declare this word means, both transitively and intransitively, **"to be rich, to make extremely rich."** Note well at this point that the purpose of God's grace in this passage is that this "abounding" of "making extremely rich" might come our way.

Next, look at the expression, "God is able." Unlike Abraham, we know God is "able." Our problem is still "will" He? Furthermore, the way this is translated, "God is able," doesn't help us unravel this knotty question of "will He?," either. This translation, "God is able," makes it look like God's "ability," here, is contingent upon something. Since the translation "God is able" is silent as to whether or not it is His will to make us "abound" it makes His "ability" look like it is contingent upon *it being His will.* In other words, this translation demonstrates that God has the capability to make us extremely blessed, but it doesn't answer the question, "Is this His will"?

I hear people all the time say, "I know God has the ability (is able), to bless me financially. But is that His will?" I hear people all the time say, "I know God is able to heal my body. But is that His will?" Furthermore, this translation, on the surface, doesn't appear to answer the question, "Is it God's will to make me abundantly blessed?" But we shall see momentarily that this translation is woefully inadequate.

Here is what the Greek text actually says. See the little word "is"? This word "is" is not in the Greek text. It is in italics in your Bible which simply means that it was added by the translators to make the meaning clearer. But this addition of "is" in italics, muddies the water to the point where we cannot tell what this verse actually says. In the preceding paragraph we saw that the addition of "is" makes it appear that God's being "able" is contingent upon His "will." ***But, when we eliminate "is" we eliminate the contingency aspect of it.***

Let's demonstrate this by taking a closer look at this word translated "able." The Greek root from which comes this translation "able" is the Greek root from which comes our English word "dynamite." Literally, this word means "power, explosive power." It means "dynamic." It is translated in its various forms in our English Bible by the words "power," "authority," and "able." Vine's says it means to "show yourself powerful." Furthermore this word "dynamite" is a Greek present active indicative verb. The indicative mood, as it is in English, is the mood of reality. It's the mood which states the actual and the real. In addition, we must note that the Greek present means "continuous action in present time." Therefore, the present tense, combined here with the indicative, states what God is really, actually, continuously doing now, *contingent upon nothing, including His will.* Based on the above, here is how our verse literally reads.

> **8 And God is continuously showing himself powerful by POWER-ING UP AND DYNAMITING all grace toward you TO MAKE YOU EXTREMELY BLESSED; that ye, always having all sufficiency in all things, may abound to every good work:**

To put it another way, God, by his powerful grace, IS MAKING you extremely blessed, CONTINUOUSLY.

> **8 And God, IS CONTINUOUSLY MAKING YOU EXTREMELY BLESSED by His powerhouse grace; that ye, always having all sufficiency in all things, may abound to every good work:**

In other words, *this passage says nothing concerning what God's ability is contingent upon His will.* **The Greek text, here, speaks directly about what His will is concerning wealth BASED UPON WHAT HE IS ACTUALLY DOING NOW!** This passage says that making us wealthy is something that He *is actually doing NOW.* God *is* "dynamiting" His grace to continually make us blessed and prosperous now. This is the Greek present active indicative used here.

God *is* powering up His grace to us for the purpose of blessing us. It's not just something that He is capable of doing. It's something that He *is* actually doing. In other words, blessing us is something that God *is actually doing* for us with His powerful, dynamite grace. The Greek text will not support the idea that this is something that He *might* do if only it was His will. We can't read that into this verse. That's not in there.

He really is actually doing it. Therefore, what He plainly states that He *is actually* doing, is most definitely His *will.* We don't have to worry about knowing God's will concerning blessings. It is God's *will* for His all powerful grace to make you prosperous. It is indicative. It's reality. It's actual. God *is continuously* powering up all grace toward us to make us extremely blessed now. Why *is* He doing this? For what purpose *is* He continuously doing this? To answer this question, we must get to the second part of our verse which reads thus:

> **that ye, always having all sufficiency in all things, may abound to every good work:**

This is a Greek purpose clause which answers why God is making you extremely blessed. Now understand, Greek purpose clauses operate by strict rules. Greek is the most exact language known to man. New Testament Greek was not as exact as classical, but, it's still more exact than any language on earth today. So, these purpose clauses operate by very strict rules. "That ye" literally means in Greek "in order that ye."

In other words, God is making us extremely blessed "in order that" something might happen. This "something" will give us the purpose of why God is "dynamiting" His grace on our behalf. I like that. God is "dynamiting" all grace for us. God is "powering up" and "dynamiting" all grace for us. Why? Purpose clause! "In order that, in order that, in order that" you always having all sufficiency in all things, may abound (be extremely blessed) to every good work.

Notice something extremely important here. "In order that" designates why God is dynamiting all grace to us. It says why He is doing it; so that you "always having all sufficiency." Look at the word "sufficiency." This is a word that comes from the Greek verb ARKEO which means "to ward off" or "to defend against." That word is used about a dozen times in the Greek New Testament. Whether the verb form or the noun form is used, without exception, *it always means to ward off or to defend against a hardship caused by the lack of something.* A lot of people worry and wonder if God ever took away the apostle Paul's thorn. God absolutely did take away Paul's thorn, because when Jesus said to Paul, "My Grace is sufficient for thee," He used the same word, "ARKEO." It is translated "sufficient." What that means is this: "Paul, I am going to defend you against that thorn. I am going to ward that thing off for you." This statement is in the Greek present tense which means continuous action in present time. Therefore, Jesus Christ not only got rid of that thing, but He kept on getting rid of it for the rest of Paul's life.

Also in verse 8, the word "sufficient" means "to ward off" and "to defend against." So what this passage is saying here is this: God is dynamiting all this grace to us for a twofold purpose. The first part of His purpose is this: in nothing will there ever be a hardship created by lack of anything. He is dynamiting all of this powerful grace to you so that you might be sufficient and have all these adverse consequences, (caused by lack of something) warded off of you. The second part of His purpose in making you extremely blessed is this: He does it so that you might abound to every good work.

111

Previously, we noted the word "abound" translates a Greek word which means "abundance," "more than enough," "to make extremely rich or wealthy" and "to overflow." God is dynamiting all grace so that it "abounds" towards you. In other words, "so that it continuously makes you extremely blessed." The word "abound" is used twice. God will "power up" all grace toward us in such a way that all His grace will overflow us. God will give us an overflow. God will not just give us enough. He will give us an overflow.

It's like the grace of God is contained in a giant water tank sitting up on a tower. There is enough water in that water tank to totally supply an entire town and a valley. When the need arises, God will dynamite that thing so that we will be caught in a flood of overflowing grace. There is so much grace that will come from God that will just flood over us. Out of that flood, that overflow, all the adversity caused by the lack of anything, will be swept away, and therefore, I am totally self-sufficient by the powerhouse grace of God. Hallelujah! Out of that overflow from God He wants me to take what I need and then He wants me to take some of that overflow and be an overflow myself to every good work.

God deals with you through His grace. His overflowing. *But He deals with good works through you.* God gives His grace directly to you. But He wants His good works supported through you taking some of that overflow and overflowing to the good works. Giving is like planting a seed. If you sow sparingly, you will reap sparingly. If you sow bountifully, you will also reap bountifully. 2 Corinthians 9:6-7 says:

2 Cor 9:6-7
> **6 But this I say, He which soweth sparingly shall reap also sparingly; and he which soweth bountifully shall reap also bountifully.**
> **7 Every man according as he purposeth in his heart, so let him give;**

not grudgingly, or of necessity: for God loveth a cheerful giver. (KJV)

Then verse 7 says for us to determine the purpose of our giving. It says "as he purposes in his heart, so let him give." Purposes what in his heart? Purposes the kind of harvest he needs. If he needs a big harvest, give a big seed planting. Everybody has some seed. If God has given you any kind of a job, that's overflowing grace. If you doubt that, ask the guy that doesn't have one. It's overflowing grace. Out of that overflowing grace, your needs are being met and you have an abundance leftover to support and overflow to good works. Out of those overflows, we are to plant some more seeds in the various, different good works. They must be good works. We saw previously that "abound" means to "make someone extremely blessed." Therefore, out of our overflow, we are to make every good work "extremely blessed" so they will be able to minister to others without hindrance.

As you give your seed to make good works "extremely blessed," that seed is going to come back to you. You are going to reap much more than you sowed. I say this not out of law. There is no law involved. I am saying this so you can prosper. For when you, out of your overflow, begin to support and plant seeds in these various good works, that seed will come back 30, 60, 100-fold. You see, when God set up this economic system, He gave an overflow out of which two things are to happen. First, you are to be totally self-sufficient. You are to have absolutely no adversities caused by lack of anything.

Second, you will have the ability to overflow to other good works. That is what that verse says. You are to have no lack; that's what God has already set up and has running. If in fact, it is not operating like that for you, do you know what happened? You blocked up the dam.

Do you know how you blocked up the dam? You won't hear or if you hear, you won't receive it, and when you don't receive it, you measure it. You put measures on it. You put limits on it. Any time you do that you slow up the flow. And when you slow up the flow, your reaping will suffer. Therefore, you must open up the dam by giving or planting the proper amount of seed. It's out of God's overflow that you are making an overflow of your own. And as you give a part of that overflow to the good works, God will bless you.

Can I give you a personal experience that demonstrates the above? Once, there was a person I know that needed a few bucks, and I knew they needed it then. The Spirit of God just said to me, "Give that person some money now," and told me how much. I gave this individual $100. Two days later, there was a person who came up to me and said the Spirit of God spoke to me and said for me to give you this.

That person gave me an envelope. I opened that envelope and there was $300 in it. Before I even opened the envelope, the Spirit of God said "You really needed that $100 you gave that person the other day, didn't you?" I said, "Yes." So I got the envelope and opened it and He said, "Do you still want your $100 back?" Do you see how this works? There's no need for anybody reading these pages to be up against it financially. The only reason we are up against it financially is we have not been planning for the proper harvest.

If you want to reap a harvest – a consistent, healthy, balanced harvest – you don't plant a seed and skip thirty feet and plant another one when you ought to be planting something about every nine inches; because as you plant, you are determining the harvest you are going to reap. You know we have too many "Burger King" Christians. We all want it our way. You know they say "Come to Burger King and we will make it your way." Well, you see we all want it our way. But remember this, only a dummy is going to eat up his own seed.

114

If we do it the way God said do it, we are going to have (1.) no adversity created by lack in anything. That is what that word "sufficient" means. You can check this in any Greek Lexicon. It means to "ward off" and "to defend against." It is always translated by some form of the word "sufficient." It means "to ward off and to defend us against an adversity caused by the lack of something." (2.) We will have an abundant overflow of grace demonstrating there is no lack that can ever occur to you. (3.) Out of that overflow He wants you to set up your own little overflow, *for the overflow you set up determines from that day forward the amount of overflow that comes back to you.*

For the overflow you set up determines from that day on the amount of overflow that God makes come back to you. Jesus said the good ground hears and receives what it hears without putting limits on it. When you hear and receive without putting limits on the Word, that means you are going to act on it to the fullest. That person will receive the hundred-fold. Period. Concerning prosperity for us as Christians, He has a set of rules we *must* play by. It will be to our folly if we don't.

If you will hear me and receive what I have said to you without limits and measures and act on it, the hundred-fold reaping is guaranteed to you. You will have no lack in any area of your life. The Bible says God is dynamiting all grace to the overflowing point of making us extremely blessed. Remember the Greek purpose clause. You are to have no adverse consequences caused by lack in anything so that you might overflow to every good work.

There are many "good works." So, get serious about it and ask, "Lord, which good work do you want me to overflow to?" Perhaps He will tell you to make TBN extremely blessed. Perhaps He will tell you to make a book, tape, and healing ministry like this one extremely blessed. Perhaps it will be an evangelist or a missionary. But He will tell you about those he wants you to make extremely blessed. When He tells you which one(s), then ask Him, "How much?" You will be blessed and prosper beyond anything you ever thought possible: thirty, sixty, or one hundred-fold. I am not talking about 100% return on the money. I am talking about one hundred times the amount of the investment. Now that's heavy. Am I right? I gave $100, I got back $300. Isn't that beautiful? But, this is the exciting part! I have already sown another $100 of that $300. Plus, I'm not through reaping from the first $100 yet. Pretty soon, it is just going to build itself into something like a snowball rolling downhill. It is going to be an overflow. That's how it works. That's what God said.

Father, in the Name of Jesus bless us now financially. Amen.

Chapter Eight

More Proof That Abrahamic Blessings And Provision Belong To You Now

John 10:16 is the story of the sheepfold. Let me explain some things about this verse, and then I am going to look at this chapter beginning with verse one. But it is imperative that we understand verse 16 first.

> **John 10:16**
> **16 And other sheep I have, which are not of this fold: them also I must bring, and they shall hear my voice; and there shall be one fold, and one shepherd. (KJV)**

Now I want you to look at the English word, "fold," which is used twice in this verse. The first time it is used, it is the Greek word for "fold," AULE, and it should have been translated "fold." Some of your Bibles may have that as a footnote. The second occurrence of the English word "fold" in this verse is a totally different Greek word from the first one that is translated "fold."

This second occurrence, however, should NOT have been translated "fold," because it is the Greek word for "flock," POIMAN. There is a difference in a "sheepfold" and "a flock of sheep." These words are radically different in the Greek and should have been so translated. I don't know why they were translated like this. As a matter of fact, a lot of theological errors have been brought about by this translation. What this verse actually says is this: "Other sheep I have that are not of this fold." That is what it says. "Them also I must bring and they shall hear My Voice and there shall be one flock composed of two

117

different groups of sheep." Now having said that, we will go to chapter 10 and read the first six verses.

> **John 10:1-6**
> **1 Verily, verily, I say unto you, He that entereth not by the door into the sheepfold, but climbeth up some other way, the same is a thief and a robber.**
> **2 But he that entereth in by the door is the shepherd of the sheep.**
> **3 To him the porter openeth; and the sheep hear his voice: and he calleth his own sheep by name, and leadeth them out.**
> **4 And when he putteth forth his own sheep, he goeth before them, and the sheep follow him: for they know his voice.**
> **5 And a stranger will they not follow, but will flee from him: for they know not the voice of strangers.**
> **6 This parable spake Jesus unto them: but they understood not what things they were which he spake unto them. (KJV)**

The word "verily" is a translation of a Greek word from which comes our English word "amen" and it means "truly." When somebody says something in the preaching and some one of you says "amen," what that actually says is "I agree with what you are saying because what you are saying is the truth." This translates the Greek word "amen" which means "truly."

The flock and sheepfold is the typical scenario of something with which everybody in that day would have been familiar. It was the scenario of the sheepfold. A sheepfold was a place usually in a valley which had been built and fenced so that the shepherds from the surrounding hills might bring their flocks in there at night for safekeeping. When they would go in there, all these sheep, belonging to various shepherds, were mixed together. Back then, they didn't have name tags, they didn't have branding irons, like we do today. They just mixed all the sheep up in this one huge corral, as it were, which was a sheepfold.

But there was something unique about the relationship of the sheep to their individual shepherds. The shepherd and the sheep got to know each other. They got to know each other to the point where the shepherd knew the sheep's names. And the sheep knew the shepherd to the point where they recognized his voice, and they would only respond to their own shepherd.

It didn't matter if there were 500 sheep in the sheepfold, the next morning when it was time for the shepherd to take the sheep out and go back to the pasture, he could get in there and begin to call his own sheep by name and one by one they would come out of the other 500 even though that particular shepherd might have only had 6 or 8 sheep. They recognized their own shepherd's voice. They responded to their own shepherd's voice. They came out and all the other sheep would stay there. They would only come out when their shepherd came and called them out of the rest of them.

This is the scenario here and there is not one thing unusual about this passage. This is how it was in the Middle East at that time. This is a typical shepherd language, word-picture scenario. All the sheep, belonging to the different shepherds having come down from the hills, would be placed into the sheepfold at night.

The individual sheep, however, would only follow their own shepherd. This means I could go in there and I could call out your sheep and they would never respond. You could go down there and call out my sheep and my sheep would never respond to you. My sheep would only respond to the sound of my voice. This is Jesus' meaning in the following verse.

John 10:27
27 My sheep hear my voice, and I know them, and they follow me:
(KJV)

119

Jesus claims two things here for himself as He speaks this scenario to these people. He says, first of all, "I am the Door." And second, not only is He the Door, but Jesus says He is the "Shepherd." Third, He says, "I have some sheep in there. I have a flock in there." But then He says "I have some sheep of another flock that are not in there yet. I am going to bring them and put them in that sheepfold and I am going to make one flock out of two."

When Jesus spoke, Christianity didn't exist yet. They were still operating under what? Judaism, which operated under what? The Abrahamic Covenant. The Abrahamic Covenant included healing, prosperity, well-being for their families, in addition to the salvation of their souls. Jesus is saying, "That is My flock in there, but I have a flock out there that hasn't been brought in yet." What's He talking about when He says "another flock"?

He is talking about bringing the Gentiles into the only "fold" God ever had, which is the Abrahamic Sheepfold. What Jesus is setting the stage for is to bring the Gentiles into the Jewish flock, into the Father's fold, the fences of which are composed of the Abrahamic Covenant. If we put all this together, this is how we come out. If we lift everything out of context, nothing makes sense and you can make it say anything that you want it to, but when you do, you will absolutely lose your healing, your prosperity and your well-being, because these three things are contained only in the Abrahamic Covenant Sheepfold.

The sheep that He already had in the fold were Jewish sheep. Those people obviously were under the Abrahamic Covenant. But when He says, "I have other sheep that are not part of this flock that I want to bring in. I am going to put them into the flock which is located within this fold." He's bringing us Gentiles into the same Abrahamic system.

120

You know what the great mystery about the church was? Dispensationalists say the mystery of the church is the fact that it was hidden in the Old Testament, that they didn't even know anything about a church back then. But that's not what the Bible says. The great mystery of the church in the Old Testament was the fact that Gentiles were going to be grafted into the same Abrahamic, Jewish system on an identical, even basis and even footing with the Jews, so we have everything going for us that they had going for them because we are now in their Abrahamic system.

So Jesus said, "I have sheep which are not of this flock that I am going to put into the same flock inside that fold, and like the bunch of Jewish sheep, the Gentile sheep are also going to respond only to my voice. Then there will only be one fold and one flock, one door, and one shepherd." At that point, Gentiles become a part of the Jewish fold who had healing and prosperity and well-being for their families promised to them. And we Gentiles are going to be put into the same flock inside that same fold. That fold has never yet been changed by the Hand of God. That's where we Gentiles are.

Jesus said He was the Door. He also said He was the Shepherd. Then He contrasted Himself to a thief and a hireling.

John 10:7-15
7 Then said Jesus unto them again, Verily, verily, I say unto you, I am the door of the sheep.
8 All that ever came before me are thieves and robbers: but the sheep did not hear them.
9 I am the door: by me if any man enter in, he shall be saved, and shall go in and out, and find pasture.
10 The thief cometh not, but for to steal, and to kill, and to destroy: I am come that they might have life, and they might have it more abundantly.
11 I am the good shepherd: the good shepherd giveth his life for the sheep

12 But he that is an hireling, and not the shepherd, whose own the sheep are not, seeth the wolf coming, and leaveth the sheep, and fleeth: and the wolf catcheth them, and scattereth the sheep.
13 The hireling fleeth, because he is an hireling, and careth not for the sheep.
14 I am the good shepherd, and know my sheep, and am known of mine.
15 As the Father knoweth me, even so know I the Father: and I lay down my life for the sheep. (KJV)

That same principle can be applied to the ministry. A lot of preachers today could care less about their people. They are in it purely because it is their career. They are nothing but a bunch of hirelings. When the pressure comes on and the going gets rough, those people will jump ship and give their people over to the wolves. They could care less as long as they make their number one objective, which is climbing the political ladder of their career.

I took a man's place in a church one time, and right after I got there the former pastor came to town and wanted to take me to lunch. So I went to lunch. All that I could hear was about this man's career. He was worried about his career, how his leaving the church in bad shape before I got there, how it was going to affect his career. It was his career this, and his career that, and his career something else. I was sitting there saying to myself, "This guy is a hireling. This guy is a hireling. This guy is a hireling." Not one time did he ever say to me that he was concerned about the church, that he was concerned about the sheep, that he was concerned about the flock.

He was worried about his career. The guy's a hireling. Are you listening to me? Jesus said the hireling will dump the sheep because he doesn't care for the sheep. He is more concerned about what he is going to put into his pocket than he is about the sheep. Brother, Jesus has no confidence or use for a religious hireling. They are professional clergymen. They dot our landscape from coast-to-coast in this country, and they are an abomination to God Almighty. There is no power in those ministries. There is no power in those churches, because they are hirelings.

Jesus said "I am the Good Shepherd and I will lay down My life for the sheep." When you have somebody who is willing to lay it on the line, he will do that. Jesus said "all that ever came before Me was a thief or a hireling." They didn't care. All they wanted was what they could get, what they could put in their pocket. They were for sale. But He said, "I came that My sheep might have a more abundant life." Notice what He said. I give My life for the sheep that the sheep might have the abundant life, not Himself.

There is a radical difference between the hireling and the "real McCoy." It doesn't take a whole lot of brains to figure it out. That's like the two women who got into an argument over a child. They both said, "The child belongs to me." And they went to King Solomon to settle the problem. One woman finally gave the baby up because Solomon was going to cut the baby in two and give half to one and half to the other. The one that was the real mother said, "No, give it to the other woman." Why? Because she had a greater concern for the child than she did for herself. You see, the hireling could care less. He wants what he can get. But the shepherd will lay his life down. And, a genuine sheep can sense this, because a real sheep only follows the voice of the real shepherd. He does not respond to the voice of a thief.

Jesus said not only am I the Shepherd, but I am the Door and all this bunch that has come before Me are nothing but thieves. Then He said these so-called shepherds that come around here are nothing but hirelings. They are in it for what they can get. They don't care about the welfare of the flock. But the shepherd gives his life for the flock.

Where am I going with all of this? It's amazing to me that everybody here can know that God loved us enough to give His Son, Jesus. Jesus loved us enough to give His life. But they think, "They don't love us enough to give us anything else we might need." When Romans 8:32 says, very simply, very quickly, and very plainly that:

> **Rom 8:32**
> **32 He that spared not his own Son, but delivered him up for us all, how shall he not with him also freely give us all things? (KJV)**

How can that be? In other words, anything that I have need of, I am entitled to look to God to have that need supplied because it only makes sense that God will give it to me since He cared enough to give me His Son. The Son, being the Shepherd of the Sheep, laid down His life for me.

It only makes sense to me that I can expect the rest of the things that I might need from God to be forthcoming since this has already been done in my behalf. Do you see the logic that I am following? Let's look at the Shepherd giving His life for his sheep:

> **John 10:17-18**
> **17 Therefore doth my Father love me, because I lay down my life, that I might take it again**
> **18 No man taketh it from me, but I lay it down of myself. I have power to lay it down, and I have power to take it again. This commandment have I received of my Father. (KJV)**

You see, Jesus did not have to do what He did. No power on this earth could have taken His life. God promised Him that. But He laid down His life because He had the power to do it and the power to pick it up again. But nothing else had power to take it away from Him. That is the love of a shepherd. Do you see where I am coming from? If God cared enough to give up His Son, and the Son cared

124

enough to deliberately give up His own life, how could it ever be possible for God to not, along with Him, also freely give us all things. If there is ever a need in my life, a bill that I cannot pay, surely I could go to God and expect to get some help. If ever a sickness came along that I needed some help with, surely if all of this other stuff had been invested in me by God the Father, and God the Son, surely I could expect help from God. Are you seeing this?

This is a real Shepherd. He gave His life. If He gave that, surely He will give us the paltry things: a healing, and extra few bucks, to help us make it. That is the difference between the Shepherd and the hireling. Jesus was not for sale. I mean you couldn't blackmail Him and scare Him. Nobody had power to take anything from Him. He had the power to lay His life down and the power to take it up again, and He deliberately chose to do what He did. He did that because He loved us. That's the real thing. That's the distinction between a hireling and the real thing. Aren't you glad we serve the real thing? Aren't you glad that God still has some real things in this world? We don't have to get suckered up with a hireling. I can't stand a person that is for sale. You know that old expression, "Every man has his price." Don't you bet on that. There's some that don't. I mean there are some that you can't buy with any amount of money. So don't say every man has his price. Every man does not have a price, because not every man is for sale. I mean sometimes you choose between climbing the political ladder for your so-called career and between doing what's right. Most of the time, these two things are radically different. The hireling will go the ladder climbing route, but the real thing will stay on the bottom rung if it's necessary, because he is not for sale.

Are you a hireling? Or, are you the real stuff? There comes a time when you draw a line in the dirt, and do not step across it because you are going to serve God no matter what. Now if you haven't come to that place yet, sooner or later you will. When you do, you best draw the line because you cannot walk down both sides of that fence at the same time. The hireling will. He doesn't care where he lands. He will go on the side that pays him best. But the real thing will stay on the bottom rung of that ladder until Jesus comes, if that's what's necessary, because he is not for sale.

Do you know that most churches would be a whole lot bigger if they would just cater to certain elements? If the pastors would run over to people's houses and hold their hands and do this and do that, they would be a whole lot bigger. But it would be a great big nursery.

Father, bless this day. Bless this humble exposition of Your Word. Thank You my Father that through the Good Shepherd You brought us Gentiles into the flock of God, into the sheepfold where there with them now there is one flock, not Jew and Gentile, there's one. And we have been grafted into the Jewish structure which is the Abrahamic Covenant. Therefore, healing and prosperity belong to us and we thank You.

Chapter Nine

The Wealth of The Sinner
Is Laid Up For The Just

In Deuteronomy 8:17, God is saying some things through Moses to the Abrahamic Seed Group. Keep in mind that what is said to the Abrahamic Seed Group pertains to us Christians because we are grafted into that same group. So he is saying for us to be careful about saying in our heart that our power and the might of our hand has gotten us this wealth.

> **Deut 8:17**
> **17 And thou say in thine heart, My power and the might of mine hand hath gotten me this wealth. (KJV)**

This is a word of caution about the source of what we have. You see, God is speaking through the pen, the mouth and the ministry of Moses, a warning to the children of Israel who, at that point in time, were the Abrahamic Seed Group.

Keep in mind, however, that we're grafted into these words as Gentile Christians. We're now part of this. He's saying, "Be careful lest you say in your heart that you did it, that my power, my mind, my sharpness, my hard work, and my abilities are responsible for my gathering and accumulating the wealth that I have." Because at this point, they were beginning to be very, very wealthy. And in verse 18, God says:

> **Deut 8:18**

18 But thou shalt remember the LORD thy God: for it is he that giveth thee power to get wealth, that he may establish his covenant which he sware unto thy fathers, as it is this day. (KJV)

Do you see that God is the one that gave those people the power to get wealth? Yeah, you're pretty sharp. Most of you have probably better than average jobs. I mean you are one shrewd cookie. But the Bible says that God is the One that gave you the ability and the power to get the wealth that you are presently accumulating. The question is, "Why did God do that?" Keep in mind, again, this is written to the Abrahamic Seed Group. Now church, who is this bunch called the Abrahamic Seed Group? They are the members of the church and the church dates all the way back to Genesis 12 when God called Abraham and made a covenant with him.

That's the church. The church was composed of Abraham's seed then and now. When we Gentiles get saved, we're grafted into that same identical Abrahamic system. Therefore, what he says there applies to us also because we are grafted in. So he said it is God that gives you the power to accumulate wealth. The question is, "Why did God do that?" Look at the rest of the verse and you will see. He did it so He might establish His covenant which He swore unto the fathers. The fathers are Abraham, Isaac, and Jacob. But look at the word "established." "Established" translates a Hebrew word which is uniformly translated by our English word "continue." It is a fact that God was speaking to a group of people who lived over 400 years after Abraham did. It was a fact that He had to establish the Abrahamic Covenant with this group of people because they were Abraham's physical seed which we call in this work, *The Abrahamic Seed Group*. But, He "established" it with them by way of "continuing" it. So the word "established" really means in this context, "to continue." So God is saying, "I gave you power to get wealth so that I might simply continue the promises that I made to your father Abraham."

128

Now then, I answered my question. Why did God give us power to get wealth? Because He promised that ability to Abraham and to his seed. Well, we Christians are Abraham's seed. Therefore, that ability to receive the wealth that God spoke of includes us because we are present day Abrahamic Seed Group. So then, the Bible says that God has given us the ability to get wealth so that He might continue the promises that He made to our father Abraham. Now having said that, let's turn to the book of Proverbs, chapter 10, verse 22.

> **Prov 10:22**
> **22 The blessing of the LORD, it maketh rich, and he addeth no sorrow with it. (KJV)**

"The blessing of the Lord, it maketh rich." Now you see I have absolutely no qualms about believing that God wants his people, not just to get by, but absolutely to be rich. That's what He said to Abraham. And it says here that, "The blessing of the Lord, it maketh rich." Does it say it maketh you tend to poverty? Does it say the blessing of the Lord maketh you not have enough? Does it say the blessing of the Lord maketh you as poor as Job's turkey? You know, I used to honestly believe that there was not a way in the world for anybody to be right with God if they had a dime in their pocket and had a decent car to drive and decent clothes to wear.

Then one day I got to thinking, you know, every time my car breaks down or I look and see a hole in the bottom of my shoe, not only does it not make me close to God, it makes me fiery mad. I can't be spiritual with a car that won't run. I mean I lose my spirit quickly over a car that won't run. When a car won't start, I will trade it in a flash. I will trade a car that won't start even if it's just a battery. I'll get rid of the whole mess. I don't believe God is in anything like that.

But I honestly believed that for me to be right with God I had to be in near poverty. And I know a lot of churches that believe that about their pastors. They believe they have to keep that pastor down and out to keep him right with God. And, of course, keeping him right with God makes them feel right with God, so they welcome the opportunity to keep him in poverty that much more. I don't believe that anymore. What does the Bible say? "The blessing of the Lord, it maketh rich." Do you see that? So then I am blessed because I'm Abraham's seed, and I'm getting richer by the day and I make no bones about it. I don't have one need in this world.

Not only does the blessing of the Lord make rich, but notice the balance of the verse. *"He addeth no sorrow to it."* Do you see that? He addeth no sorrow. I know folk that go around all their lives wanting to get under some kind of martyr situation. Well, I'm not the least bit interested in being under a martyr situation. I have no qualms about thinking that God doesn't deal in martyred sorrow. I think God wants his people to be healthy, and I think He wants them to be wealthy, and I think He wants a song in their heart, and a smile on their face and a spring in their step. Because when God is doing business with you He adds no sorrow with the blessing He sends that makes you rich. Now, if that's the case, where then, does sorrow come from? It doesn't come from God because His blessings make rich and He doesn't send sorrow with His blessings. So if you are sorrowful today, guess where you got that? You surely didn't get it from God. You see, this is for the Abrahamic Seed Group. Do you see why I was so happy when God revealed to me about His Abrahamic Covenant and the fact that I'm in it? I'm happy because I figured out what all God had promised me. And He said, "My blessing makes you rich. And I did that just to keep My covenant going which I made with Abraham and into which you, Christian, are grafted now." And He said "In addition to that, I don't send sorrow in my blessing."

Now, friend, I want to tell you something. I don't know what brand of Christianity you've been following, but I don't follow this sorrowful kind of Christianity. I don't believe it's necessary to be poor to be right with God. The Bible says the "goodness of God leadeth thee to repentance," not the poverty of God.

Rom 2:4
4 Or despisest thou the riches of his goodness and forbearance and longsuffering; not knowing that the goodness of God leadeth thee to repentance? (KJV)

I don't need to be poor as Job's turkey to repent. That doesn't get me to repent, it makes me mad and I get worse. I get on a treadmill going down, and the best way for me to get off that thing is go buy a new shirt and tie and be sure my car runs good because if it doesn't, I'll trade it. Why? Because the blessing of the Lord maketh rich. And God sends no sorrow with it. I'm not in the sorrowing business. Isn't this good news? The word "gospel" means, from the Greek language, "good news." No wonder.

The thing that bugs me is, for so many years of my life, they didn't tell me all the good news. They told me I could get saved and go to heaven and that was good news. But the balance of what they had me to believe was the fact that I was on my own, twisting in the wind. I shouldn't expect God to bless me with a little financial help when I needed it. But that's not the case. The Bible says the blessing of the Lord maketh rich and God sends no sorrow with it. That's written to The Abrahamic Seed Group of which I'm a part. Now let me show you some things about giving and receiving. Look in Proverbs chapter 11, verse 24.

Prov 11:24
24 There is that scattereth, and yet increaseth; and there is that withholdeth more than is meet, but it tendeth to poverty. (KJV)

Here is something that absolutely doesn't make a bit of sense, but it works. There is he that scattereth and yet increases. Now, this is weird. How can I scatter and get rid of what I have and yet by scattering increase what I had to start with? That's like saying to me that if I have a gallon jug full of milk and I pour it on the ground and then look back at my jug, its got more than when I started. That doesn't make sense. But it works. Will you do it in the name of the Lord? There is he that scattereth and yet increaseth. That is the hardest lesson for a Christian to learn. That is the toughest thing in this world for us to learn: by scattering we get more. There is he that scattereth yet he increaseth.

Notice the next part of the verse. And there is he that withholdeth more than is fitting, but his withholding or his savings tendeth to poverty. God has a miraculous way of doing business that defies the laws of logic. But the thing that is striking about it is this: when you try it, it works. The fact that you can analyze it and test it is logical, and once you check it out, it is also "spiritually logical" because God said it would work.

So we have some opposites here. There is he that scattereth but he ends up with more. Then, there is the man who saves every dime he can get his hands on. I mean he will pinch a nickel till the buffalo hollers. But, what he's doing tendeth to poverty. I had someone say to me the other day, "Do you know what I noticed about you, Jay?" I said, "What?" He said, "You don't eat your seed." I thought about that. I said to myself, "No, I don't, but I wonder where this guy is coming from?" I said, "What do you mean?" And he said, "When you get these books printed, it costs several thousand dollars, doesn't it?" I said, "Yes, it does." And he said, "You got the money to keep printing new books from other book sales, didn't you?" I said, "Yes, I did." He said, "In other words, you use the book sales as seed money to do more to get your book ministry out there, and by

scattering you now have more books than you had when you started."
There is he that scattereth but he increaseth. Now if I'd taken every
dime, stuck it in my pocket, or spent it all on myself, or saved it all
up, and sat on it, this book ministry wouldn't be where it is today.
The philosophy which says, "Get all you can, can all you get, and sit
on the can," will not work over the long haul. You see, that's the guy
that withholds or saves more than really is necessary. Your Bible
says "meet," "fitting" or "necessary." He saves back more than really he ought to. The guy is headed for poverty and doesn't know it.
But the one who learns to scatter is on the road to increase because
he is putting out some seed. He didn't eat his seed. He scattered it.
Now you see, God absolutely wants his people to be blessed.

Prov 11:25
25 The liberal soul shall be made fat: and he that watereth shall be
watered also himself. (KJV)

He says in verse 25, the liberal soul or, giving soul, shall be made fat
and he that watereth shall be watered also himself. The guy that
learns to give will be made fat from the hand of God. It's not talking
about calories; it's talking about your pocketbook. That's the fat he's
talking about. And the one that watereth is going to be watered again
by the hand of God. What I'm trying to say is this: When you begin
to understand who you are and what the promises of God are to you,
and you begin to abide by those promises and live by those promises, you will find that God becomes responsible for you. You are not
on your own anymore. You don't have to hack it out by yourself anymore. God has now made Himself responsible for you and he begins
calling the shots in your behalf. Therefore, he that learns to water,
God is going to water him. So, my job is to go around watering
things that need to be watered, not thinking about my own need for
water because if I take care of the watering ministry God has given

to me through my giving, then God Almighty is going to water my needs Himself. And the liberal soul, the Bible says, shall be made fat by the hand of God. But, the key words here are "liberal soul." I have to learn to get liberal. I have to stop being "pinchy." I have to stop getting all I can, canning all I get, and sitting on the can. I must learn to scatter and water so that I can be watered and increased. Do you see this? By my learning to be liberal with my scattering, watering, and giving, then I become fat. Not because of myself but because of what God does for me.

These are promises that God made to the Abrahamic Seed Group. If you have named the name of Jesus Christ as your Savior, you are part of the Abrahamic Seed Group. Notice something else in verse 26.

> **Prov 11:26**
> **26 He that withholdeth corn, the people shall curse him: but blessing shall be upon the head of him that selleth it. (KJV)**

He that withholdeth grain the people shall curse him; but blessing shall be upon the head of them that selleth it. In other words, I have something that people need, and I refuse to sell it to them. (Here it's not even talking about *giving* something, it's talking about my refusal to sell it.) If I have something that this whole community needs, why would I not sell it? So I can drive the price up. But if there is a need and I refuse to sell to meet their need in order to corner the market and drive the price up, the Bible says that people will curse me. And surely they should. But, if I provide for the needs of the community, not by giving (in this context), but by selling it at a fair price, or at least making it available when it is mine to control the distribution of it, the Bible says the same people that would curse me if I withheld the necessary merchandise will now bless me.

You see, God does not operate by the laws of man. Everything I'm saying here defies human logic. But everything I'm saying here works because it is backed by the *supernaturalness* of God Himself. Let me show you one more thing in the book of Proverbs, chapter 13 and verse 22.

Prov 13:22
22 A good man leaveth and inheritance to his children's children: and the wealth of the sinner is laid up for the just. (KJV)

"The wealth of the sinner is laid up for the just." That means there's a lot of wealthy devils out there that have lots of my money because I'm the "*just.*" *I am.* And I think collection day is here. "The wealth of the sinner is laid up for the just." Somehow God brings about a transfer of wealth so that the sinners take their wealth and give it to me and to you because it's mine and yours to start with. The Bible says the wealth of this world belongs to God anyway. The cattle on a thousand hills are His. Even the thousand hills are His. Therefore, the cattle are also His. If I own the hill I own the cows. Even our laws say that possession is nine-tenths of the law. If I own the hill, I'll put a fence on it and what's in it is mine. This is the law of "eminent domain." If you study law or real estate you'll find our laws make those same statements. So God has it all. What the evil people have, really, is His wealth to start with. Furthermore, the Bible says it's all laid up for the just. I'm learning more about who I am everyday of my life. I'm Abraham's Seed and I've done my best to communicate that to you so you can understand who you are, what your rights are, and what God's promises are to you, so you can begin to have that which belongs to you.

God is the one that gave us the power to accumulate wealth. We need to stop saying that I'm going to this and I'm going to that and I did this and I did that. We need to say that God gave me the power to get wealth for one reason: He promised wealth to Abraham and He's giving it to me to continue the covenant He made with Abraham. Why modern theology removed the Abrahamic Covenant from its teaching and preaching, mystifies me. I won't let you forget about it because God does not want us to forget about it. So then, the blessing of the Lord maketh rich and God sends no sorrow with it. God is not in the sorrowing business. God is in the provision business. God is in the blessing business. As soon as we learn this and move out in it, these blessings are going to accrue to us. I'm longing for the transfer of wealth from the wicked to the just. That's what I'm looking for and it's happening. I've had people come up to me who were just outright reprobates, and God laid it on their heart and they said, "I'm supposed to give you this," and they'd give me $15.00 or $20.00 or $100.00 or whatever it was. That's a wealth transfer. Why'd they do that? They don't know why they did that. In the past, I didn't know why, but I do now. They can't help it because their wealth is laid up for me. And God has them give me some of it. "The wealth of the wicked is laid up for the just." "Just" means cleared of all guilt. That applies only to Christians, the seed of Abraham.

So, my people, listen to me. Let's throw off this poverty mindset. Let's begin to think in terms of who we are and what God has promised to us. And let's begin to think in terms of "giving in order to get" because the Bible teaches it. Let's begin to think about scattering in order to increase. Let's begin to think about "if I save more than I should, it tendeth toward poverty." And yet, God said His blessings are intended and designed with riches in mind and sorrow is not added with it by God. I didn't write these Scriptures, I just told you what they said.

Father in heaven, in the name of Jesus, bless this humble exposition of your Word. Teach us, our Father, to give in order that Your blessings might be put in gear so we might obtain. Heavenly Father, it is not Your will that sorrow come with Your blessings. You don't do that. Help us, O Lord, to see that with You there is no sorrow, that we're your children, that You love us and want to bless us and make us prosper. And You do this to keep Your promise to Abraham. Bless our people. Free us, O Lord, of this poverty mindset. Free us, Father, from the blinders of tradition that most of us grew up with. And teach us, O Lord, to do business Your way so that You might bless us Your way. In Jesus Name. Amen.